❦ Reviews ❦

What People are Saying

RoxAnn is one of those people that I knew I wanted to have as a lifelong friend from the moment we met. I have now known her for almost seventeen years. RoxAnn is the definition of a beautiful person who truly loves others. Within the pages of this book, you will discover the life in the lessons. She shares lessons such as, "When I set a boundary, I am saying, 'No' to unhealthy people and saying, 'Yes' to new opportunities," and, "Once I learned how to forgive myself, I was able to change the way I looked at myself."

This book is heart-rending and draws the tears out of your eyes, but it never once loses the message of redemption and hope. For every tear there is a lifted head and a laugh as RoxAnn overcomes unimaginable obstacles through faith and courage and learns how to love herself and others as God does.

Deborah Henne

Speaker and Author of *Gentleness: It's Not What You Think*
deborahhenne.com

This little treasure is packed with courage, truth, and wisdom. The RoxAnn I have come to know and love the last ten years is a prayer warrior, a servant-leader, a good listener, a kind, generous and supportive wife, mom, friend, and woman of God. RoxAnn's story is a beautiful example of the transformational power of the Gospel. Walking with her through the struggles, hardships, and life lessons she has experienced has brought my heart great encouragement and inspiration and I know it will do the same for you. God never wastes our pain. I am so thrilled to see the redemption this book represents.

Kate Griffin
Pastor at Allison Park Church
Owner/Founder of Pittsburgh School of the Arts

Knowing RoxAnn for twenty-five years, I had not yet heard her incredible testimony in its entirety. Her intensely honest words will cause you to laugh, smile, cry, wince, & sometimes audibly gasp. She unashamedly details her journey from brokenness to beauty as a loving and patient God performs a supernatural transformation in this willing vessel. RoxAnn is a wonderful example of Eph. 3:20. (TPT) *Never doubt God's mighty power to work in you and accomplish all this. He will achieve infinitely more than your greatest request, your most unbelievable dream, and exceed your wildest imagination! He will outdo them all, for his miraculous power constantly energizes you.*

God continues to use her wisdom, gifts and talents in various ways to minister wholeness to others. If you are not a stranger to adversity and longing to be made whole, I know these words will bring hope and healing to you.

Rev. June Gunst

Learning to put the FUN in Dysfunctional

Life Lessons from RoxAnn without an "E"

Learning to put the FUN in Dysfunctional

Life Lessons from RoxAnn without an "E"

Written by
RoxAnn Gallagher

With Amy Travis

www.amytravisunlimited.com/fusion-publishing-group

Unless indicated otherwise, all Scripture quotations are taken from
The Holy Bible, New International Version® NIV® Copyright
©1973, 1978, 1984, 2011 by Biblica, Inc.® Used by permission. All
rights reserved worldwide.

Scripture quotations marked (ESV) are taken from the ESV® Bible
(The Holy Bible, English Standard Version®), Text Edition: 2016,
copyright © 2001 by Crossway, a publishing ministry of Good News
Publishers. Used by permission. All rights reserved.

ISBN 978-1-7335626-7-6

Printed in the United States of America

Published by Fusion Publishing Group
Butler, Pennsylvania 16002

Edited by Mindi Stearns, Printworthy Proofreading

Dedication

To my husband, Keith Gallagher, the man who showed me commitment and unconditional love, just like Jesus. Always and forever, Babe ♥

Table of Contents

Learning to put the FUN in Dysfunctional

Life Lessons from RoxAnn without an "E"

Acknowledgments

I am so grateful for so many people that God has placed in my life that have spoken encouragement and life into me. I can't possibly list everyone because there are so many. I just wanted to list a couple people that made the biggest impact on me.

Thank you, Keith, for helping me make this book a reality. I couldn't have done it without your support.

I'd like to acknowledge my maternal Grandma Mary Garczewski—our prayer warrior. Thank you for always praying for me and your family. When you passed away in 2010 at 95, I remember saying that I hope that I can leave such a legacy of love like you had done for your family. I will try my best to carry that torch.

I would like to thank my friend Renee (Jenkins) Bucker and the Jenkins family for showing me what a family should look like. I tried my very best to model that in my own family.

Thank you, Nancy Miller, for showing me how to be a nurturing mom!

Thank you, Judy Dillalogue, for the countless times we got together in our homes or on the phone and for being that friend where "iron sharpens iron," as the Bible says.

Also, I would like to thank Betty Pala for all her wisdom and compassion which she always gave me during my healing process throughout the years.

Thank you to all the ladies that attended the Bible studies that I went to and/or led at church, in our homes, and even at the Eat-n-Park parking lot in a car. No one can mess with a praying mom—that's for sure. We will pray anywhere at any time.

I am grateful for April Foster from Breaking Chains Ministry in Belgium for showing me what missionaries do each and every day, miles and miles away from their families, in order to pursue the call God has given them. Missionaries are such a unique people, and I am grateful for all of them.

I am grateful for all the people God sent in my life to be a thorn piercing my soul. Because of them I learned how to forgive and how to pray through it.

Also, I am thankful for all the messages that I have listened to from so many pastors and Christian speakers. They put so much time into their calling. They are not perfect, but they just keep preaching and sharing all the knowledge God has given them. I am grateful for the Holy Spirit's prompting to take me out of my comfort zone so many times, including the writing of this book. Every time I am stretched, I am being molded and becoming more like Jesus that's what we are all called to be like.

Thank you, Amy Travis, for being obedient and placing your Facebook post just at the right time. Because of that post and all of your help, my book became a reality.

In conclusion I want to say a prayer to all those who read this book. May God bless you and keep you and may His face shine upon you and give you peace.

Introduction

I have been on this journey of life sixty years this September, and I have always wanted to tell my story. Growing up in the '60s and '70s, there wasn't much information or help available for young women trapped in dysfunctional situations, like myself. I can look back now and even laugh about some of the hard times our family went through. Laughter proved to be good medicine for me.

I'm happy to report that my life has been transformed. Even though I experienced trauma throughout my life, I am healthy enough to help others in need. As my own story unfolds, you will see that my ministry is a calling from God. He has taken my own pain and used it for His glory and His people who are currently suffering. I am not unscathed from my experiences, but I have taken what happened to me and turned it into something beneficial. I have dedicated the rest of my life to helping anyone I can, in any way that I can. This ranges from small gestures like a hug, to big gestures like traveling to another country. I go wherever God calls me.

By the grace of God, I have become a spiritually, mentally, and emotionally stable woman of God, and a prayer warrior for my family and friends. I have ministered to many women of all ages throughout my lifetime. My ministry extends to sick and homeless people on the streets of Pittsburgh to New York City and even from Belgium to the continent of Africa.

During the last seven years I have been involved in ministries helping victims of human sex trafficking. When

I found out about these ministries, I couldn't start soon enough. *Breaking Chains Network* in Belgium delivers hope and freedom to those who are trafficked in the Red Light Districts of Antwerp and Brussels. Closer to home, *Living in Liberty* provides a safe house and work opportunities for women who have been trafficked.

I prepared myself for working at the safe house by reading many books on this subject, going to conferences, and listening to teachings. I have assisted by taking ladies to therapist appointments, shopping with them to buy an outfit for court, cleaning and painting rooms at the house, and just sitting and listening to them. Being present goes a long way. And so do hugs.

God made me a sensitive person. This sensitivity has given me the ability to show compassion towards others. I learned the hard way that by not setting boundaries—the kind that protects your heart—everyone else's pain and trauma affects you. If you don't take precautions, you will burn out. Boundaries and I have a love-hate relationship. Admittedly, this has been probably my biggest challenge.

But as I've grown, I no longer allow other people's problems to suck the life out of me. I have learned to give them to God. It is His job, not mine. He has shown me that "I AM GOD" and "YOU ARE NOT."

I have learned so much from the people God has placed in my life: friends, pastors, and even from other victims of trauma and abuse. I have read many books from others who have shared their own stories. I am now a nurturing, loving, person. Sometimes when I look back I think, *wow, is this really me?* I have learned to love myself with the same love that God gives. People have told me that they love how genuine I am. I am one of those people who wear their heart on their sleeve. What you see is what you get. I have encountered many people, throughout my life, who have mentioned to me that I am funny, kind, compassionate, giving, and now full of wisdom. I was not always like this.

I am blessed with a wonderful husband, Keith, going on forty years this January. We have two beautiful adult children, their wonderful spouses, and six beautiful grandchildren ranging from twenty-one years to a year-and-a-half. Our son Kevin and his wife Kristina have three beautiful girls: Elizabeth, Emma, and Ellyana. Our daughter Kaleena and husband Kevin McLaine have three handsome boys: Grayson, Colton, and Austin. (Since our son AND son-in-law are both named Kevin, it is sometimes crazy to figure out which Kevin we are talking about.) There is nothing better than being grandparents! What a blessing our family has been in our lives.

●●————————●●

The journey of writing my life's story started when I was a child. I love to write and always have. If you took the countless journals I've filled, I would probably have enough information to write several books. I have even written poems, songs, and short stories about events in my life.

Several events have happened in the past six years, however, which pushed me closer to publishing my personal story as a ministry tool to help others. In 2015, I went through a nine-month program for training through our church called the Northeast Ministry School. Participants received a certification upon successful completion and the course culminated with a trip to Africa. All of our training prepared us to work at a five-day festival through SOS Missions. The purpose of the trip was to preach the gospel to the unreached people groups who have never heard the salvation message of Jesus Christ. We also distributed supplies for children and provided medical services for some of the sicknesses which are common in Africa.

During the interview to get into this school, a wonderful lady name Barb Trbusic prayed for me. During the prayer she said something that struck a chord, *"RoxAnn, you have something to say, and people are going to listen."* I knew in my heart that this was something directly from God and not anything I would come up with on my own. These words lit a fire in me. I knew that something was going to happen. I had no idea how that would unfold at the time.

I remember thinking *what do these words mean? Will anyone really hear me? Am I going to be visible so that everyone would hear my heart? What could I really say that would be so profound that people would listen to me?* This one statement prompted so many questions in my head. I thought that something was going to happen while I was in ministry school, but nothing really stood out. Still her words remained stuck in my mind like glue.

And then last year I knew I was going to write a book to tell the story.

While I had Covid in November 2020, the desire to write kept getting stronger and stronger. I slept so much during the first week but would wake up with different thoughts in my head. As I prayed, names of the chapters came to my mind. I made notes so that I could begin writing once I felt better. But after a few months I became discouraged because nothing was happening. My husband knew how badly I wanted to write a book and how the writer's block had me really down. One day when I was particularly frustrated with myself, my husband Keith said, "I will be back," and left to go to the store. When he returned, he handed me a bag. In the bag were ten notebooks and a pack of different colored pens for writing. What a sweet gesture!

I knew I didn't have any excuses, but I still wasn't sure what to do next. I think Covid had made my mind so foggy and I was still so tired that I couldn't think straight. The frustration continued to mount as I would see on Facebook how many of my friends were publishing books. I know I'm not supposed to compare myself to others, but it was driving me crazy! I knew that I could do it, but had no idea where to start. All the memories in my head made it difficult to know what direction I should take. Should I ask someone? Yes. I can focus, but sometimes my mind is all over the place. Every song I heard, smell I smelled, movie I watched, and event I attended triggered different memories, and I didn't know how to organize them all in a way that would make sense to someone else. My brain was on overload.

Around this time, I came across a Facebook post that spoke directly to what I was thinking. It said something like, "Have you ever wanted to write a book and didn't know how to start or where to go?" This post was from my friend Amy Travis who has recently released a book and started a writing mentorship program to help people write their own story. Wow! The timing of this post was amazing, and I immediately responded. Within weeks I met with Amy, and she helped me put all of my stories into categories and chapters. She listened to me for four hours as I rambled on about the stories of my personal life. Thank God she was patient and kind.

Before I knew it, I was sitting at the computer WRITING MY BOOK. I'm sure nearly everyone who has ever wanted to write a book wonders the same things: *Can I do this? Is my story worth telling? Will anyone even read it?* But I kept writing anyway.

My motivation is to genuinely help others; I don't do anything out of guilt or shame. My life's crisis has catapulted me to want to help others and let them know that they do not have to suffer alone. I am not a certified therapist. I do not have a degree in anything, but I **DO** have life experience. Although I still struggle, I have learned how to get past some of the trauma. By doing so I can recognize that my past does not reflect my present or future, but it does allow me to help others in seemingly hopeless situations.

I've learned that I can still function, even when surrounded by dysfunction. That's my prayer for you too.

1

Crisis of Identity

For the first sixteen years of my life, I spelled my name "Roxanne," even though that's not the spelling of my name on my birth certificate. I've often wondered...*how does that even happen? Why was I not taught how to spell my name the correct way?* If it were not for my consumer business class teacher in high school, Mrs. Alberta Kelly, I would have probably spelled my name that way for the rest of my life.

You will see how throughout my early life there were many situations which contributed to a crisis of identity for me.

I came from a very large family. My mom's family was Polish, and my dad's side of the family was Italian/English. I grew up in the '60s and '70s when most families lived in close proximity to each other. We lived in a city neighborhood where I could walk out of my door and walk to both of my grandmothers on both sides of the family. I also had many aunts, uncles, and cousins from my dad's side of the family who lived nearby, too.

I had such a happy life. I can remember feeling comfortable and secure with no fears at all. Everyone knew everyone, and everyone helped everyone. If you were outside playing and it was dinnertime, for example, you would eat at that family's home, no questions asked. My mom always made extra food too. I remember just being so happy.

On Sunday's we would eat at my Grandma Garczewski's house after church. She always made spaghetti with Ragu spaghetti sauce, which was a novelty during those years. You may not realize this, but Ragu originated in Rochester, NY in 1937. Assunta Cantisano and her husband Giovanni founded the Ragu® Packing Company by making their sauce. The couple made the sauce in their basement and sold it from their front porch. They later expanded to an entire factory. In 1969 the Ragu name was sold to Chesebrough-Pond which, in turn, was acquired by Unilever in 1987. This was around the time when my grandma first started serving us Ragu. It tasted so good.

We walked to school every day. Since my mom's side of the family was Catholic, we attended the Catholic School in our neighborhood. The older kids would always tell us a story about a troll that lived under a bridge we crossed each day. I always ran so fast so that the troll wouldn't get me. Perhaps that was part of my track training.

I absolutely loved going to our church, St. Phillip & James. I specifically remember receiving my First Holy Communion. When I received the host that day, I was so excited. I was sensitive to the things of God at such a young age and literally believed that the body of Christ was coming into my body. And BAM...I fell back in my seat because I passed out. My Uncle Adam picked me up and carried me outside to get some fresh air. When I look back, I can see the significance of the Holy Spirit in my life. There was a true connection from that day to my walk with God now.

Even though these were happy years for our family, there was an event which impacted my dad's sister and the entire family. My Aunt Julie's husband, we called him "Uncle Boots," died in a small airplane crash. It was the talk of the town in New Castle, PA and was all over the newspapers. It was so heartbreaking. Aunt Julie was left with six small children and no husband. This was crushing for the entire side of my dad's family.

My mom and dad, Shirley and Bill, started dating each other during their teen years. They really loved each other and were inseparable. They had to get married when my mom got pregnant with me when she was 18 years old. A little fun fact which my mom told me was that I was conceived in a corn field. Ironically, my favorite vegetable is corn on the cob. (Yes, I am laughing right now!) My parents then had my sister Morreen—which is not spelled Maureen how most people spell it. My baby sister, Louise, was born around a year later. So, my parents had three girls within three years! My mom said she used to hide in a closet some days because life was hard. She could never get enough rest.

My so-great-and-perfect life shifted when I was around nine years old when my dad and mom separated and later divorced. This comfortable, stable life was so disrupted that it created anger and resentment inside of me which lasted for years. I can remember the exact moment in my mind when I concluded that my dad's decision to leave us was my fault. I sincerely thought that for years. I can still see the back of his head as I cried out loud, *"Daddy please don't leave us!"* I remember chasing after him and the door being closed behind him. I moved the curtain off to the side and watched him go down the steps. My heart was crushed.

The memory is still very vivid in my mind because I loved my dad so much. And I still do to this day.

I have always wondered *why did I have to be in that room when he left?* I wish I would have been spared the heartbreak of watching him leave that day. That memory will be imbedded in my mind forever. As all children of broken homes can attest, it impacts you forever. I couldn't help but feel as if there had been a death in the family. The security that I once felt was gone, and I felt abandoned. Unfortunately, but not surprisingly, things got worse as time went on—not better.

I don't know that much about my dad's childhood. All I know is that his father, who he loved so much, was an alcoholic. He developed diabetes which led to his demise. When my dad's mother divorced his father, my parents took my grandfather in to live with them for a period of time. I know that had to be hard for my dad taking care of his father constantly. I'm sure that made him sad because he tried so hard to make him stop drinking.

I heard that my dad drove his father to the hospital the night he died. I believe that must have had an impact on dad's life. He now had four sisters that he felt responsible for. Losing someone at such a young age can cause so many issues in your life. There was not the same kind of help back then that there is today.

As of this writing, we really don't know why our dad left us. My mom thinks it's possibly because he wanted a boy. There is speculation that he just couldn't handle the pressure of raising a family at such a young age. It's possible that the death of his dad and his brother-in-law—both of which he loved greatly—had an impact on him and he just couldn't handle the pressure. I know grieving makes people do some crazy things sometimes.

There was a rumor floating around that my dad got another woman pregnant during this time. I heard she had a boy, and my dad was not permitted to see him because of his mistress's mother. I can see why this would put a young man in a place where he just wasn't thinking straight. As I have stated, back in the '60s and '70s there was very little help and emotional support for dealing with family issues. You just had to figure it out yourself. Or maybe help was available (after all, I found help) but he was just too proud. Pride does come before a fall. Always ask for help, no matter what your situation.

The divorce put a hole in my mom's heart too. She was devastated when the man she loved just up and left her. Here she was, caring for three young girls with no one to help her. She shared with me recently a memory she has of when she took us to church at Christmas that year. The tradition was to crawl to baby Jesus and kiss him. As she crawled, she remembers looking back at us three girls. "Here they are Lord," she prayed, "please help me with these girls because I cannot do this on my own." We just followed suit crawling to kiss the baby Jesus, just like our momma.

Our lives changed drastically when Dad left. Mom was now in a situation where she was stuck with three young girls to care for, and she really didn't know what to do. I can remember becoming "the mom" at a very young age. I can't remember if this happened naturally because of my nurturing personality, or if I was forced to help because I was the oldest. To this day, I still act like the mom at times, even to my own mom. (This is still a work in progress.)

Displaced

After some time, Mom met another guy. Looking back, my sisters and I knew she would want to be with someone else, but we had no idea how dramatically our lives would change. When she first met Fred (Bud) Upperman, I believe she thought it was a way out for us. I am pretty sure she was attracted to his strong will, which she needed at that time. Mom was mentally tired, weak, and in a very fragile state. She always believed in God and prayed for someone new to come into her life. Maybe she believed this man was an answer to her prayer.

Once my mom married Bud, he moved our family away from everything we knew and into the middle of nowhere. I no longer could walk down the street to see my mom OR dad's family. Our lives were ripped apart from everything we knew. This was more than unfair, it was devastating. Looking back, this caused abandonment issues, confusion, and lack of trust—particularly toward men.

All of the sudden, we were all displaced and disconnected to everything we knew and loved. The chord was cut so severely that we rarely saw either side of the family. We missed birthdays, holidays, and special events that you would do with a family. In fact, there were many family members who I did not get to see until I turned eighteen. Some of them I didn't see until about five years ago at my dad's side of the family's Fourth of July picnic they celebrated every year. But, as we came to understand later, this was intentional on Bud's part.

I became a very lost little girl. My sisters were younger and do not remember as much as I do, but it was traumatic for both of them also. I prayed every night that my parents would get back together again. I was in my 30's when I finally stopped praying that specific prayer. Initially I believed that God could and would do that for me. But as the years went by, I knew that it was never going to happen. I remember sitting down as an adult and telling my mom about my prayer and that I had finally let that go. I cried really hard, but my mom didn't belittle me about it. I think she understood how I felt. Although this prayer was not answered exactly how I intended, God brought us all back together again in a beautiful way. I'll share that story later in the book.

It wasn't until much later that we realized just how much baggage Daddy Upperman (as we called Bud) brought to the relationship too. Bud did not have a great childhood and suffered his own crisis at a young age. He was a fighter in both senses, physically and mentally. He struggled with school, and he didn't graduate. Because he got into trouble all the time, Bud ended up in a George Junior Juvenile Detention for stealing. We're not sure what type of abuse he may have experienced during that time, but this had an impact on him which changed his life forever.

To add insult to injury, his family left him in the detention for an entire extra year! I can picture his family sitting around and asking each other, "Where is Buddy?" I can't imagine how that would affect a young person. It's no wonder he had abandonment issues.

As a result, Bud was a bully who always had to defend himself. My stepdad had so many insecurities and strongholds which caused wrongful thinking. Even on his deathbed it became clear that he couldn't shake this insecurity. I remember him telling my mom that he loved her, but then he brought up the fact that she would probably go back to her ex after he died! I can't imagine what causes a person to think like that.

Daddy Upperman often talked about his momma, though. He loved her very much. One time I played a song for him from my phone to show him the cool feature of typing a song or phrase in to find a specific song. He had tears in his eyes when the song played.

"What's going on?" I asked. He said that it reminded him of his mom. As I think back, he must have had so much pent up hurt which shows me how—even in dysfunction—love always finds its way into your heart.

My Old-New Identity

To return to the story at the beginning of this chapter … During my consumer business class, Mrs. Kelly was teaching us about checking accounts and how to fill out a check using pretend ones for the class. I remember asking her how to sign my name. "You write your name as it appears on your birth certificate," she told us. I went home that day and asked my mom if I could see my birth certificate.

After inspecting the document, she handed to me. I distinctly remember yelling out "Mom, what the heck??" The lettering on my birth certificate was not even close to how I was taught to spell Roxanne! I couldn't believe it. The name on my birth certificate said "Rox Ann." There was no "e" and a space between "Rox" and "Ann."

With this discovery, I began spelling my name "RoxAnn." (I don't add the space for everyday usage, but my passport and driver's license have a space.)

Although this incident at sixteen years old wasn't the beginning of my identity crisis, it sure didn't help. I was a high school sophomore at the time and ran track. Fortunately, I was good enough to get my name in the newspaper. Actually, my name was in the paper every week during the track season. Even though I was a little embarrassed, I went to speak with Tom Spudic, the sports editor from our local newspaper who followed our high school track team. I became familiar with his face since he was always at our track meets.

All those years my name was spelled with an "e". I talked to him, explained the situation, and asked if he could correct my name on any future articles. I know this was a crazy request and I wonder what he thought. Tom was very kind and honored my request. It's funny looking back now and seeing all my sports paraphernalia. Prior to that year, all of the newspaper clippings, trophies, etc., show my name spelled with an "e" at the end.

Over time I realized that I wasn't the only one suffering from an identity crisis—my mother, father, and stepfather each had their demons to contend with. I can see now how my mom may have forgotten how she spelled my name on my birth certificate.

The dysfunction that my stepfather brought into our family carried over into my own life, as well. His insecurities caused so many arguments between him and my mom which affected me as a child. For example, my mom was not allowed to have any contact with my dad, my biological father, Bill. It would be decades—and after Bud's death—before my mom and dad could even be in the same room.

This man caused so much unnecessary pain and hurt in all of our lives, as you will soon discover.

2

Crisis of Fear

I was in fifth grade when we first moved to the little town of Bessemer. Moving from the city to a very secluded farm area wasn't all bad because we could play outside. The owner of the house had acres and acres of land that he farmed. Some years he grew corn, and some years he grew oats. I was a happy camper to walk outside my door and pick the corn on the cob. We could have as much as we wanted. We adjusted to this new life by tending to a garden and taking care of the chickens we raised from an incubator. We also had ducks and horses to take care of. The outhouse we had to use, on the other hand, took some adjusting to for this city girl. Most children are very resilient to new environments. We were well taken care of with the things that we needed: clothes, food, and lots of space to explore.

I remember learning that a local girl had drowned in the quarry right before we arrived. Many of the students at school were talking about that. Since it was a small town, everyone knew her and talked about what a nice girl she was. Because I've always had a sensitive spirit, I was really sad even though I had never met her.

It was difficult as a new student to find my place, but I started to make some new friends. I met a girl in my class named Renee and we are still good friends today. There was something special about her; she had a great personality and was friends with everyone. I remember going over to her house to play, and I just wanted to stay there forever. Her mom would occasionally invite me to stay for dinner. Her family had something that our family lacked, and they made such an impact on my life. Often, I would imagine that they were my family...even if it was just for that day.

Renee didn't have the kind of fears that I had. It was at this point that I started to recognize that something wasn't right. Since then, I have had so many moments when I have looked back and realized that my thoughts and actions were not normal.

I can't really tell you exactly when the irrational fear started to come into our lives. There was a mixture of some good days and some not so good days. I don't know why my stepdad kept a shotgun beside the couch all the time. Was he afraid someone was going to come into the house and rob us? I don't know if that was the case, but he constantly used that shotgun to threaten us. As a child, it is hard to tell when someone is joking or serious. I cannot even tell you how many times he would cock his gun as if he were going to shoot us. It was his way to get us to behave, even if we weren't doing anything bad at the time. In fact, we were pretty good girls and didn't misbehave very often.

Every day I thought could be the day we were going to die. When my stepdad would come home from work, we didn't know what kind of mood he was going to be in. His actions were so unsettling, but we eventually learned how we could manipulate the situation. If we were pretending to do chores, for instance, he would leave us alone. I would carry around a rag in my hand and a can of Pledge® while he was home. My sisters and I could never be caught just sitting down or watching TV.

One day my stepfather asked which of us girls took the change from the back of the toilet. My sisters both said they didn't. I felt really badly about lying to him and telling him I didn't, because I did—but I didn't want to die that day. He was so angry that he grabbed a chain saw and started it up! My poor little sister Louise saw him running up the steps with the saw on and confessed that she took the change. It's possible that she could have taken some change, but I knew that I definitely did. But once she confessed, he turned off the chain saw. I was so terrified that I have absolutely no recollection of what happened next.

I don't know where my mom was when all of these things happened. All I know is I never allowed that to happen to my sisters again. I became more protective of them than ever before.

Living in fear every day put such a toll on our lives and it gave us so much anxiety. I started having problems swallowing food because of my nerves. On many occasions Bud made me stand up against the wall and hold my uneaten food in my hand until it was all gone. I really don't know how long I had to stand there, but it was a cruel punishment.

On the positive side, my ability to problem solve grew exponentially. I can walk into any situation and find better ways of doing things. On that specific day, I was holding meatballs, so I pulled up my pant leg and put the meatballs in my socks. He came in to inspect that I had eaten them and then told me to go to bed. I remember thinking to myself, I hope that he doesn't check my clothing or I am going to die. I just could not eat the food. Thank God that I did not develop any eating disorders as I got older.

During another occasion, I don't remember exactly what happened, but we were all at the table eating dinner in our small kitchen when the situation escalated quickly. The conversation was going fine, or so I thought, until my little sister said something. For no apparent reason, my stepdad threw a saltshaker at her and hit her in the head. She started to bleed and got a big bump on her head. I honestly don't think he meant to hit her on the head. He just meant to throw it past her, but why was he throwing a saltshaker at her in the first place? What could an eleven-year-old say to him that was so terrible?

I did not like my stepdad at all, but I excused that as a rational thought that every child has. I mean, why would any child like their stepparent? Most children just want their mom or dad and know that the individual can never truly replace their father or mother. I felt very justified in my anger toward him and thought it was perfectly normal.

Holidays were the hardest on our family because of all the dysfunction. I remember my mom was making turkey for Thanksgiving Day for the first time. She had never made one before. Just when we were ready to sit down to eat, my stepdad found out that my mom left the insides in the turkey—like the neck and gizzard. He was so mad that he picked up the whole pan and threw it out the door.

He proceeded to call my mom all kinds of names. It was terrible.

Trapped

While writing this book, I discovered that my stepdad never liked the holidays because his own father left him, his mom, and his siblings on Christmas Eve. As a result, this was NOT the happiest time of the year for us. One year we were coming home on Christmas Eve after visiting relatives and he could not get the door opened to the inside of the patio that led to the kitchen. He got so mad that he grabbed my sister Louise and said he was going to knock down the door with her head! Miraculously, we found the keys right away before he could carry out his threat.

My stepdad did not like to be locked in or trapped. Apparently, he was locked in at the detention center. But even though we were able to get in the door, the next thing I knew my sister—Louise—was thrown on top of the Christmas tree. She wasn't seriously hurt that time, and we often laughed about that event. But in reality, it was not funny. It just demonstrated more irrational behavior. I think the reason we all laughed about those times when we were growing up was because if we didn't, we would just cry every day.

It's not surprising that one of the more traumatic events of my childhood happened on Christmas Eve. My mom and stepdad were fighting about something (I don't even remember what) while we were driving to the city of New Castle to see my Grandma Garczewski. My sisters and I were sitting in the back seat with no seat belts, because we weren't required to wear them at that time. I could hear them screaming at each other as we came around the bend and then—all of the sudden—Bud hits the gas pedal and wasn't letting up! He drove through the parking lot of a little ice cream stand and just floored it. I thought to myself, oh my God, we are going to end up in the lake! I thought for sure we were going to die that day. He stopped right before we hit the water.

Dear Lord, what was this guy doing? Christmas is supposed to be a time of celebrating with family. It shouldn't be full of fear thinking that we are going to die that day. I remember he was drinking peppermint schnapps that day, so whenever someone is drinking that particular alcohol, or I see a creek or a bridge, or we are driving around a sharp bend, it triggers anxiety in me.

It wasn't until I became an adult and saw a therapist that I realized how some of the things that he had done to us as children caused PTSD. I thought PTSD was only for soldiers returning from war. But the counselor put a label on it for me when she talked about how certain images, noises, or odors can trigger anxiety in me. She also reassured me that those things that happened to my sisters and me were not normal.

I can't go back into this man's mind and try to figure out the cause of this dysfunctional behavior, but my stepdad must have been dealing with his own irrational thoughts while he was raising us. I often wondered if he was angry because he had left his first wife and four children and ended up having to raise us three girls. I am speculating because to this day I cannot even begin to think of the "whys." My mom told me that he hated women. I always wondered if someone hurt him while he was left at the detention home. How ironic that he had to be with four women really.

He wasn't very kind to his own sister, either. I remember a situation when Bud called my mom to pick him up at a local bar. She had no idea what she was getting herself into that day. All three of us girls were in the back seat once again. Bud yelled at mom to get out of the car and told us not to look back behind the car. All I could hear was screaming and fighting. All of the sudden, I could hear the thud of flesh being hit. My stepdad beat the crap out of his sister because he thought that she was a lesbian and that was his way of disciplining her. Mom tried to get in the middle, but he pushed her out of the way. He actually broke my aunt's jaw! She could not eat for two months. My aunt never pressed charges.

If these situations happened today, he would have been charged with assault on multiple occasions. It was a different time, and many things were overlooked back then. In the end, my mom, my aunt, and others would learn to forgive my stepdad and have meaningful relationships, but things didn't look good at the time. As a child in the back seat, yet again, I thought that my aunt was going to die, and we would be next.

Another question that was always in the back of my mind was…Where was my real dad and why couldn't I spend that time with him? To add to the irony, my stepdad had four of his own children and they felt the same way that we did. Why was their dad raising another man's children? My biological dad ended up raising three girls from his new wife. Even though I had no resentment towards the girls, I couldn't understand why he could raise them, but he couldn't raise us.

The fear from being abandoned by my own father was so hard on me as a child. As an adult, I can look back with a little bit of understanding and—believe it or not—I have compassion for both my dad and stepdad. I know it doesn't seem rational, but when you begin to mature and you look back at your own wrongdoings, you find that you can have dysfunctional compassion. I don't even think that's a word—I just made it up!

My stepfather's anger was not just reserved for his family, either. One day he beat up a guy who was delivering a microwave to our house. For some unknown reason, Bud suspected that he and my mom were having an affair. He walked outside, punched the guy, and called Sears to complain about the delivery. This kind of behavior put up a wall in my heart that I was not ever going to let anyone treat me like that when I got older. My goodness...he was just delivering a microwave.

To this day, I always struggle with men coming to my house to do work when I'm home, whether it's an electrician, plumber, or the cable guy. I am not afraid of the men—I am afraid of the unknown of what they might do to me. I know that it is an irrational way to think, but my stepdad left me believing that men are disgusting and everyone just wants to have sex with me. His constant insecurities began to create a misconstrued idea of what men were like.

There were many days when I wondered why my mom wouldn't leave him. One time, my mom and stepdad had gone away for the weekend to a motorcycle rally. When they came back, my mom had a motorcycle tire mark on her leg and she was in a lot of pain. We came to find out that Bud was mad at her and HE RAN HER OVER with his motorcycle. I didn't understand why she stayed. My mom said that she tried to leave him on so many occasions, but he would always beg her to come back.

We all lived in "flight stage" for many, many years. My mom said they didn't have women's shelters or places where she could have gone at that time. These are just a few of the horrible things that I can remember. Although I don't wish to go into all of the details for the sake of my mom and sisters, there was sexual abuse and the fear of being sexually abused. I can tell you, however, that it does mess with your mind as a child. I learned to put a wall up for protection so that I would not be hurt again.

Thankfully, there is not the stigma of sexual abuse now that there was back then. Many people have a platform and voice to share their experiences and help other women in these situations. If we were in this situation today, I'm confident that my sisters, mom, and I would be able to find help.

Sexual abuse is very prevalent today, too. Unfortunately, I believe many women are in this situation. The good news is that more people are aware of this situation, and more avenues are available to find help. When we were younger, no one talked about it. If they did talk about it, it was a hush-hush situation. Other people knew what my family members were doing but no one said a word.

3

Crisis of Self-Sabotage

I was around twelve years old when my stepdad became angry one day and—out of the blue—told Morreen and me to go outside and take off all of our clothes. At least, that's what we thought he said. We ran out of the house as fast as we could, and we did exactly what he said. Even though it was winter and really cold outside, we stood on the porch with no clothes on. Our entire bodies were exposed, and I remember being very humiliated and cold. I thought maybe we would be executed like this and die. My youngest sister recalls grabbing our clothes and throwing them to us out the patio window.

My mom said that she couldn't believe her eyes. Bud looked at her and said, "Why are your children standing outside with no clothes on?"

I don't know if he told us that or not, but we thought we heard him say that, so we did it. It's possible he said something else, but we lived in such fear that if we thought we were told to do something, we did it—even if it was wrong. Bud laughed about that for years saying that he couldn't believe that we were standing outside with no clothes on. In some ways it is funny, especially if he didn't say that, but no one really knows what happened that day or why. We learned to be compliant and did what he said.

I can't even imagine what my mom was thinking. I believe she was pretty numb and just concerned with surviving. She felt trapped with nowhere to go. I would imagine that she carried around a lot of guilt over that, too. My mom took care of our physical needs but not our emotional needs. She couldn't because she was just as afraid and abused as we were.

It didn't take me long to understand that being compliant made my life a lot easier. I obsessed about doing the right things and always kept my room spotless. After moving to Bessemer with my stepdad, I developed OCD (obsessive-compulsive disorder) and became a perfectionist. This tendency always existed as part of my personality, but the desire became more heightened out of fear. Sometimes when my mom and stepdad would leave for the day to do errands, I would clean the house instead of playing. What kid would even think to do that? I would dust the whole living room and clean the wood paneling using the oily furniture polish. When I cleaned, I felt like I was in control of the situation. The best part of cleaning came in the form of affirmation when my mom would come home. She always said "thank you" and told me how great the house looked. I just wanted to make everyone happy.

As time progressed, I began to take on the role of a mother for my younger sisters more and more. Mom spent some time in the mental ward at the hospital in those days, so I was the mom at home. Because I was a people pleaser by nature, I always tried to care for and protect my sisters as best as I could. The first time I left the house for school, both of my sisters grabbed onto one of my legs and wouldn't let go. I told them that I had to go to school and I would be back home. I will never forget that day. A part of me was excited to be going to school, but the downside to perfectionism, I soon realized, is that you recognize that you can't always be perfect. This created a different type of fear in me. I became angry knowing that I would never be able to attain that perfection. That anger was always right below the surface, so every mistake I made brought it out.

Thankfully, I found an outlet for all of my energy and perfectionism—running. Even as a child I was faster than most kids my age or older. If someone chased me, they were not able to catch me. When people found out that I was really a fast runner, they encouraged me to join the track team at school. This provided some much needed affirmation for me. Finally I discovered something I was good at. Joining the track team was such a reprieve for me. It got me away from the house, even if it was for a couple of hours.

As a freshman in high school, my coach saw something in me. Mr. David Bredl was a great coach and gave us all such confidence that we could do better. We wanted to do better for him. He said that I had a lot of natural ability and was easy to coach. Even so, he showed us how to be more efficient and trained us to work hard. He taught us how to take off times from our races and add distance to our field events. Mr. Bredl just retired a couple years ago!

By my junior year I was really excelling and had a chance to make the State tournament. As the end of the season approached, my team gave me a huge card which they all signed as a way to encourage and push me to do my best. I received numerous ribbons, medals, trophies, and plaques throughout my track career, but the highlight was winning the 400-meter dash at States my junior year. Running was, and still is, something that I could control. I am still surprised that I was allowed to run track. It's even more shocking that my stepdad let me stay out of town for a few days when my team went to States. I remember having to hide that card in between my mattress for a whole year before I was able to take it with me to college. I still have it today.

Graduating from Home

By the time I was graduating high school, all I could think was *I can't wait to be on my own*. Some of my friends didn't want to leave their cushiony life, but I was so ready to leave and take charge of my own life. Even though I knew my mom and sisters were still going to live in that environment, I had to leave and not look back.

Neither my mom nor stepdad went to college, so I was on my own. My friend Renee applied to go to Clarion College, so I wanted to go there too. Her parents helped me with the application process and had taken us both to visit the school. Even though I didn't share a room with her (she roomed with another girl from high school) it provided a sense of normalcy to have her there. She was probably my main reason for attending Clarion.

My plan was to study psychology and go into social work so that I could help other people. Unfortunately, I realized quite quickly that I didn't have the discipline to be successful. As soon as I got to college and was on my own,

I began to party and do what all the rebellious kids do. I no longer wanted to be compliant.

When I was in high school, I wasn't involved in the party scene like the popular kids were. I was so afraid. I had gone to a party where they were drinking, but I immediately asked my date to take me home. I remember one time a boy called me right before I turned sixteen and because of that, my stepdad didn't allow me to get my driver's license. I didn't get my license until I was nineteen.

As I started to drink alcohol this helped me forget about all of my problems back home. I only drank on the weekends, but it was a way out of the pain and trauma... even just for a few moments. I started going to parties and it was so much fun. My roommate and I ended up having the "party room." When I started drinking at college I didn't know that it would cost me dearly.

During high school I had dated some different guys, but it never worked out. How could I even know how to be in a relationship when I was so fearful of men? But when I got to college, I became a different person. I thought I was in control, but I wasn't.

Even though I was trying to live my own life, I continued to be held captive by Daddy Upperman. Back then we didn't have the communication that we have now. My mom would write me letters and tell me what was going on at the house, and I was unable to really write back in detail out of fear he would read my letters. I tried to move on with my life, but I was always thinking about my sisters and mom and fearful that I would receive bad news one day.

I was out of control. Drinking on the weekends led to dating guys. But every time I would end the relationship because I was so afraid to have sex. I didn't even have sex until I was nineteen years old and thought that something was wrong with me. I was convinced everyone around me had already experienced that and yet, I hadn't even thought about doing it. My thoughts about relationships and sex were so abnormal because of my stepdad. I was still in the mentality that if my stepdad found out, he would come up to college and kill me.

During this time, I became a skilled manipulator. Gone were my "compliant" days. There was a guy that liked me, but I really didn't like him. I just thought of him as a friend. My roommate wanted to go to West Virginia to see her boyfriend and I told her I could take her—using this guy's car. He didn't know that we had taken it. Although I knew that there was a tiny hole in the gas tank, we started our journey. About an hour into our travels, the car stalled in the middle of nowhere. Oh no! It was so dark outside that we couldn't see three feet in front of us.

We were on the most isolated road I have ever been on, and we did not know what to do. As we started walking, we saw a light in front of us and began walking toward it. My friend and I were both so scared and held on to each other. As we approached the light, I noticed a red plastic jug on the front porch and I knew it was gasoline! We had the same kind of gas can at home for our lawnmowers. So, I was brave and ran up to the door, even though I thought the person who lived there was going to come out with his shotgun and kill us.

Even though I was afraid of being shot this provided a way out of the situation. I grabbed the gasoline and we ran as fast as we could. Once I filled up the car with the gas, we were delighted to see that the car started right up. We were on our way. As we passed the house where the container of gas was taken, I threw it out the window and yelled, "So sorry for taking your gas, but thank you anyways." I don't know how many times I put myself in harm's way during those years. This is one of those moments when I look back and I know that God's protection was on me.

But I also knew how to get my way, and I turned into a person I didn't even recognize.

Have You Seen Keith?

Keith was the first guy that I met at college. I was walking down the steps of the girls' side of the dormitory and he was down at the bottom just standing there. He had a Richland Track Team shirt on and when I saw it, I immediately stopped and pointed to his shirt. That school was where I qualified to go to the State Finals for track! So, of course, it caught my attention right away. We introduced ourselves and became friends. I can look back now and say that it was fate. Keith taught me how to drive... really drive...while we were at school. It was my best friend's mom that took me for my test though, and I am pretty sure I passed because she was such a pretty, classy lady. We laugh about that often. That was a good memory for me.

Keith started to come around a little bit more and we became more than friends. We started to do everything together. He had a girlfriend from high school, and she came to visit him one time and actually stayed with me. Keith and I had been dating but not officially. After that weekend, he broke the relationship off with her. I kept telling everyone that Keith was my brother because I was in denial of being in a relationship.

One day I came out of my bath area in a robe and Keith was sitting on my bed. He was really just a kind, innocent guy, but I was starting to feel uncomfortable and told him that I needed my space and that he was suffocating me. So, he said, "okay" and left me alone.

I can now look back on my actions and realize what I was doing—self-sabotage. I did not know how to live a normal life. If it began to look a little bit normal, I would sabotage my life unknowingly. After two weeks went by, I started to think more of Keith and missed him. I kept asking everyone "Have you seen Keith?" It turned out that he found out I was looking for him and he called me, and we started to date again.

The Ugly Cycle of Self-Sabotage

The next part of the story is very uncomfortable for me to share. I did not know what to do with this guy who was so kind and gentle towards me. Having never experienced this before, I did not know how to respond to that kind of love. You can probably guess that, of course, I was going to sabotage this relationship too.

Around this time, I started hanging out with this guy who gave me alcohol. This should have been my first clue that he was bad news. Then he seduced me into bed to have sex with him. I can remember hearing a song on the radio called "Misunderstanding" by Genesis. The lyrics said, "There must be some misunderstanding; this must be some kind of mistake." Why I didn't heed those warnings and just get up and leave, I'll never understand.

This is when I recognized that my wrong thinking was off the charts...I thought that Keith was experienced in sex, so I didn't want to feel like I didn't know what I was doing with him. How stupid was that thought? But it was a real thought. So, in my mind this guy provided a way to "practice" having sex before I could be intimate with Keith. My perfectionistic trait backfired in a big way. I was a little tipsy, but it also made me brave enough to go through with it. He was really good at it. He had a girlfriend and when she found out, she wasn't even mad at me. That did not make sense to me. She literally said he does this all the time. I later discovered that, to this guy, I was just another notch on his belt of women he had seduced.

Soon after I began to think, *Oh my God, what if I get pregnant now? What would I do?* My dysfunctional pattern of thinking led me down the road toward another bad decision. Essentially, I seduced Keith into having sex with me so that if—and when—I did get pregnant, I wouldn't have to admit the baby was someone else's. Too this day I am crushed that I could do that to someone I cared about deeply.

Because I knew I could never let a man ever hurt me again, I made sure to manipulate everything to be in my favor. I could not go through my life not knowing who the father was. I also didn't want to let out the fact that I had sex with not just one man—but two. My stepdad would kill me. A young woman in this precarious situation didn't have many options back then, or so I thought. I had been talking to a friend about my dilemma and she told me that Roe v. Wade passed in 1973. So, I looked it up. The decision was made on January 22, 1973, that by law a woman had a fundamental "right to privacy" that protects a pregnant woman's liberty to choose whether or not to have an abortion. I couldn't even think straight at that time. I wasn't into all the political parts of the abortion rights movement. All I knew was that I had a problem, and this seemed like a good solution.

After I used Keith and ended up getting pregnant, I had an abortion. I wish that I could have run to my mom, my real dad, or anyone else who could have helped me. Keith helped me to get the money and we went to Pittsburgh to get an abortion. I am telling you that it was the most awful thing that I have ever experienced, and the actual abortion caused even more trauma in my life. I caused more trauma in my own life. When I look back it makes me sad that people are still going through with this, but I know more information and better options are available. Several organizations now allow you to place a baby for adoption and receive the care that both the mom and baby need.

I sabotaged everything because I didn't know what normal was. I had no one to go to and had never felt so alone in my entire life. Even though the procedure was over, I still carried the guilt. The numbness and denial stayed with me for a long time. Soon after that, I quit school and went to live with my Grandma Garczewski. I couldn't go back home to my mom—mainly because I wasn't welcome there.

Keith and I continued to date and continued to have sex. The birth control pill I was on always made me sick. While I was at my grandma's, Keith asked me to marry him and I said yes. Shortly after that, I found myself pregnant and we had to get married. We weren't really even ready to get married. We were so young and when I think about it, I brought so much baggage to the marriage. I couldn't see it even working out. All I knew at the time was that men don't stick around.

A New Sort of Normal

Once I discovered I was pregnant, however, Keith proposed to me and I accepted. When we decided to marry I remember how supportive Keith's parents, Richard and Josephine Gallagher, were of us. The entire family embraced me with such grace and love. I knew at that moment that this family understood unconditional love.

We married on January 22, 1982, at our local justice of the peace office and had an intimate dinner with his parents and siblings. His aunt opened her home and had a reception for us, and a lot of Keith's family came and supported us.

My mom, stepdad, nor father did not come. I am pretty sure my mom and stepdad did not come because of fear of my dad being there, and my father would not come because I was pregnant before I got married. I have to mention, though, that my stepmom came—even without my dad! My Grandma Schofield was there, of course, along with my Aunt Julie. That meant so much to me to have them there. Even though it was another reminder of the depth of my family's dysfunction, I will treasure that day forever.

On July 1, 1982, we had our first child together. Back then you didn't have sonograms like you do today, so we had no idea what we were going to have. We just wanted the baby to be healthy. When we both found out at the time of birth, we both exclaimed, "It's a boy!" We named him Kevin Richard (Richard is Keith's dad's name). We were so excited.

We brought this baby home and just loved him with everything that we had. I kept records of all the things that he did, like when he first laughed and when he first crawled (he basically walked before he crawled). He was such a strong little baby. Even though we were so young and had to learn a lot by hands-on experience, this baby was ours and no one would take him from me. I discovered that both of my dads were very skeptical and didn't believe this marriage would last. As a result, I developed a chip on my shoulder because I needed to prove that this was authentic and we would last. I vowed to Keith that I would never divorce him—no matter what. I wanted to give our child the best that we could give.

We were married for about a year at this point, and everything seemed to be going well. We lived our lives and took care of our son. Soon after this, I discovered that I was pregnant yet again. After some discussion, we ended up having a second abortion. I can't even tell you why. Statistics say that most women who have one abortion will end up having more than one. Abortion is viewed as a quick and easy way to get rid of the problem. I don't have a good answer as to why we did what we did. Dear Lord, what were we thinking?

The people we are today cannot even relate to the people that we were back then. I have struggled so much as a Christian to try and understand the reasons for this behavior. The only explanation I have is "self-sabotage." All I knew to that point was dysfunction.

But then, the next time we got pregnant, we decided to keep the baby. On October 30, 1983, we met our daughter for the first time. Keith found a name from a young actor on a TV show during that year and we both loved the name, so we named her Kaleena Gallagher. Originally, Marie was to be her middle name, but my mom said she couldn't spell Kaleena so she was just going to call her Marie. Keith instantly put a stop to that and took out the name Marie.

Our little baby girl was the apple of our eye. She was so pretty and such a good baby. She was so smart, too—and still is today! We were very protective of her. Both of our children grew up and they are very close. They have two parents that gave them more love than anyone could ever have. They knew that they could come to us whenever they had need, too.

After our daughter was born, the doctor suggested that I get my tubes tied. I was only twenty-three years old. Some people today don't even start having children until after that age. I didn't question the doctor, and in some oddly peculiar way, it probably helped me to stop the cycle of pregnancies and abortions.

Even though this issue was resolved, I continued to sabotage my own life. I started to go out and do whatever I wanted. I went to bars with single friends because they had the freedom I wanted. I wanted to be single, but I couldn't because I felt stuck in my marriage. I was starting to be two different people: the RoxAnn who tried to be a mom and wife, and the RoxAnn who wanted to be the single person sowing her wild oats. My thinking was so messed up.

Now that my tubes were tied and I wasn't in danger of getting pregnant again, I had several affairs but would never talk about it. I understand now that my actions were worse than my dad's and my stepdad's.

4

The Hard Work of Healing

A traumatic event happened when we first moved into the town of Bessemer which—more than any other—plagued me the rest of my childhood and even into my adult years. One night our stepdad was screaming at us girls and made us take all of our possessions outside. Once we hauled our stuff outside, he demanded that we throw all of it on the bonfire. All of it! We watched our toys, clothes, bikes, etc., as they were consumed by the blaze. I remember having to help my sisters because some of the stuff was heavy. Everything we owned was destroyed that night.

We later discovered that the point of that exercise, in Bud's mind, was to show what a great provider HE was. He replaced everything that we owned and much more. I am not sure why our stepdad made us do some of the crazy things he did, but I can speculate that his insecurities were so crippling that he didn't want any reminder of his wife's first husband—our father. Even as young girls, we understood that he was removing us from the place where we lived to try to get rid of the memory of our father.

As you may imagine, this experience devasted me as a young girl. I specifically remember throwing away my Crissy doll. It was a doll that had beautiful red hair. You could press her belly button and the hair would get longer, and if you moved her arm backwards the hair would get shorter. This really messed me up because I had the hardest time getting rid of anything that anyone gave me—even my stepdad.

I recently realized that Bud discarded EVERYTHING that our dad had given us, including our names! Our stepdad renamed each one of us girls and never called us individually by our real names. He made up nicknames for each of us. He called me "Hudseyball," my sister Morreen "Moee," and my sister Louise "Wezey." I can't believe it took me until I began writing this book to recognize this, but I sincerely wonder if that was another way for him to literally get my dad out of his mind.

The hatred he had for my real dad must have been really bad. We had nothing that was bought for us by our mom and dad. Nothing at all. Everything burned in the fire. Of course, he replaced everything and much more, but it was a traumatic experience, nonetheless. Of all the things that happened to us, I have had the hardest time shaking this one off.

Learning to Let Go

When we were in our early teen years, I remember our stepdad taking us all to Kmart. He bought us all, even my mom, these cool winter boots that were lined with fur. Even back in the '70s these were thirty-five dollars a pair. That was a lot of money at that time. Believe it or not, I held on to those boots for over forty-five years! Our son Kevin, daughter Kaleena, and granddaughter Elizabeth wore them. We would even lend them to friends who didn't have boots when they came over to sled with our kids. I loved those boots so much that I just kept putting them away in the summer and bringing them back out in the winter. Remarkably, those boots bring back good memories for me. I could not throw them away.

So, one year when I was pulling them out of the attic, I realized that they were dry rotted and really in no condition to be worn. But I did not have the heart to throw them out—in my mind I was throwing out the good memory. When I discussed this with a friend, she suggested that I take a picture of them and then I could just look at the picture. What a great idea! But, nope, I still could not throw them away. My husband came home later that day, and I told him about my dilemma. Keith wanted to help so he picked them up and threw them away for me in the garbage can in our bedroom. Well, five minutes later I took them out and hid them under the bed! I thanked him for his kind gesture but told him I would get there—eventually.

I knew I had to throw them away myself, so finally I found the courage. I took a picture of them, as my friend suggested, and threw them in the trash. This time I did not go back after them. This was a big step for me. It's taken me a long time to be willing to get rid of anything, especially if they have sentimental value. Even though the experience of throwing all of my possessions on the fire was painful, and I can't image ever making my children do that, it made me realize that material things come and go. But what I need to invest in are things that can be stored in heaven. For example, I can be kind to someone. I can take a meal to a sick person. I can help people who need help. I always help wherever I go and try to remember those things which will have a lasting impression on those around me.

Healing Through Therapy

The first time that I ever went to a therapist I was close to forty years old. Prior to this, I had sworn off counseling because I thought that it made you weak. My mother had been in the mental ward a few times when we were growing up and I viewed that as a sign of weakness. From my younger days, I vowed that I didn't want any part of counseling or therapy. But thank God for friends who have spoken into my life. A friend advised me to go to counseling and gave me a referral for a therapist. I made the call because of her advice, and it was life changing for me.

After my initial visit, I told my therapist, "Wow, I feel really good. I don't need to even come back." I laugh now because I didn't know anything about counseling. This was the first time I had talked at that length to anyone about my childhood. I got everything out. I was surprised when the therapist said that this was just my consultation to see how she could treat me. When I was done with my consultation, my therapist looked straight at me and said, "RoxAnn, I cannot believe that you are not on drugs or alcohol because of everything you went through." I couldn't tell if that was a compliment, backhanded or otherwise. I told her it is because of the grace and mercy of God that I haven't resorted to drugs or alcohol.

Unfortunately, after seeing her for a couple of months she mentioned that she would no longer be working with adults. She wanted to help children before they became adults. I had just become comfortable sharing my information and now I would have to start over with a whole new person. This was a minor setback for me and yet, I believed in some way that it was a good thing. I wanted to see her be able to help kids at a younger age.

I have seen a few psychologists in my lifetime, and they have helped me tremendously. God has sent so many people to help me on my journey, I believe because He knew I wanted to be free. When I started counseling, I wanted to learn as much as I could. One of my therapists said that she had never seen anyone so determined to be helped. If she gave me an assignment, I would do it. Many people do not do the work to get the help they need. That would be my first advice for anyone reading this book. Do not be afraid to go to a therapist if you have any kind of trauma in your life. Do not worry what other people are going to think about you. There is no shame in taking steps to get healthy. If you do not feel comfortable with your psychologist, then find another. Even if you have to go for the rest of your life, I say GO!

About five years ago when my last therapist was retiring, she said, "RoxAnn, you are doing really well, and you don't need a therapist any longer." I felt a sense of pride as if I had graduated! I felt as if I had finally learned how to cope on my own. I can now deal with triggers as they come up. Even though circumstances and trials still present themselves, it's a new day. I've learned to thrive, in spite of the dysfunction I experienced in my childhood.

Moving on

As difficult as it may be to imagine, I believe that our stepdad loved us very much. He just did not know how to love the right way. We did have some really great days. We learned how to water ski, we had boats, and a lot of things. We had horses, and I loved riding my horse everyday with my neighbor. We learned how to take care of the animals and our garden and our yards and our homes. I learned how to sand down a car and repaint it. We had snowmobiles, motorcycles, and many bikes. Everything was maintained very well. He took pride in everything we got. We never lacked anything. But the hard days will still always be imprinted in my mind.

The boots serve as a good reminder to me that stuff is really meaningless. My sisters and I knew that we had to forgive this man and let go. Yes, it scarred each of us in different ways, but there is so much more to life than what happened to us in the past. We are all better people for going through this. This man made such an impact on our lives—the good, the bad, and the ugly. But I look back and remember the good times we had.

Throughout the remaining chapters, I'll be talking about the process of becoming emotionally healthy after years of psychological abuse. As adults we have laughed so hard and tell funny jokes about our childhood. My children and grandchildren loved him as Pappap Upperman. We all changed for the better, even him, but it was a process.

5

Overcoming Toxic Relationships

In our early married years Keith and I lived in a townhouse in a local community, so we had a lot of other young couples living near us. Most of these people had parties every weekend. In fact, I really didn't know anyone on our street that didn't drink. One of my neighbors was a young woman I worked with. We became good friends and started hitting parties and local bars together. Because I had my son when I was so young, I was feeling very lonely and trapped at this point in my life. Looking back now, it was a perfect storm.

Going to the bar to drink with my girlfriend was not a great idea. I got myself into a lot of trouble during those years. Even though this friend was an amazing person, the reality was that our relationship only fed into my unhappiness and feelings of being stuck. A few years later we moved out of the area, and I was able to remove myself from that specific relationship. I started to realize how vulnerable I had been because of the anger and all of the resentful feelings that I had as a result of my childhood.

Sadly, it took me longer than most of my friends to catch up emotionally. When you are raised in a loving, functional home one tends to learn healthy emotional habits at a younger age. When you have healthy boundaries, you are able to discern what situations may cause you harm and have the confidence to say "no." My stepdad's insecurities, however, impacted me in a profound way. My own insecurities prevented me from trusting other people. As a matter of fact, at one point in my life, I didn't even trust myself. The emotions of the little hurt girl took so long to develop into the healthy adult that I am now.

I often wondered how some people were able to handle the difficult circumstances that came their way. For me, these same situations would trigger deep depression or cause so much anxiety that I doubted I would ever be normal.

The first step in becoming emotionally healthy, in my opinion, is to remove yourself from toxic relationships. As you probably understand from reading earlier in my book, you can't always remove yourself from toxic family members, but you can learn how to set boundaries—particularly when you are no longer living in their house, under their care.

The word "toxic" has so many definitions in the dictionary. According to Thesaurus.com, here is a list of words that are synonymous with the word toxic: poisonous, destructive, lethal, dangerous, fatal, unsafe, corrupt, septic, harmful, malignant, and contaminated. A person who has toxic qualities will most likely be abusive, unsupportive, and emotionally unhealthy. This individual will try to bring you down to their level. You may begin to feel so dependent on them and their opinions that you start doubting yourself. One of the definitions of the word "toxic" is "unable to breath." Wow! A toxic person literally sucks the life out of you.

No one is exempt from being around toxic people; this happens to everyone at different degrees and at different times in your life. I often wonder why some just get stuck in it longer. I am so grateful to not be that way anymore. After spending so many of my early years in a toxic wasteland, I thank God for His grace and mercy and that I was able to get away from it.

It wasn't as simple, unfortunately, as saying, "Oh, I am just going to remove myself from these toxic people." It took many years to discern that I was one of those toxic people, and I had to learn how to take care of my inner self.

Let's just face the fact that women are emotional. If you have a husband at home and you are not emotionally stable, you can so easily jeopardize your marriage vows. When you have unforgiveness or anger issues, you leave yourself vulnerable for other men to give you attention. If you are like me, you think you can up that attention and still handle it. But, if you don't guard your heart, you could—out of nowhere—find yourself stuck in an unhealthy relationship.

Years after I had begun my relationship with Christ, I found myself in a situation where I didn't even know I was doing anything wrong. I am confident that my motives were pure. I had joined the drama team at my church, and I really enjoyed going to practice every week. My main goal was to ensure that the content of our play would help other people. I was all in for that. What started to happen to me, though, was that the drama teacher—a younger male—began giving me emotional attention. I must admit, I liked that feeling. I didn't see anything wrong with it.

At this time in our lives, my husband and I had already gone through forgiving one another and our relationship was at a healthy place. But, seemingly out of the blue, he made a comment to me one day and said, "Hey, do I have to worry about this guy and you?" The question really surprised me, and I said, "No, he is just a nice guy." But the more I thought about it, the more I could see how easily a woman like me could find herself attracted to another man because of the attention. Women, please be very careful who you give your emotions to.

That entire situation was a learning experience for me because I didn't even see it coming. I share this with you now because it happened so quickly. But because I had a loving husband and his statement was not belittling or angry, I was able to see my vulnerability and not allow myself to become trapped in an emotional affair. He asked a very wise question.

I discovered that setting boundaries for myself— primarily when dealing with toxic people—is so important. When I set a boundary, I am saying, "No" to unhealthy people and saying "Yes" to new opportunities. I remember a lady praying for me a long time ago when I was a new Christian. She laid her hands on my shoulders from behind and said to me, "Let your yes be yes and your no be no." I didn't even understand at the time that the statement was directly from the Bible, but that word stayed with me for many years. I learned how my decisions impacted my life and those around me. I also learned that having healthy boundaries set me free so that I could be a better person and could help others, too. Once you learn how to say "no" to people and situations which endanger your mental health, you can begin to help others who are not as healthy.

Toxic people are hard to deal with. I have come to learn that some people will never listen to your wisdom or heed your advice for various reasons. First of all, they don't think they have a problem. Secondly, they are so involved in their own destructive thinking that it would take a miracle from God for them to change. Often, people have to learn things the hard way. You cannot force a person to do anything, even if it is for their own benefit. We can be there for them when their world is falling apart after they have made their decisions. That has been one of the hardest things for me to do—sit back, pray, and wait for them to ask for help. Some of them never do. Many of them continue to live with unforgiveness and pain.

In my own life, I have found that the biggest asset to becoming a better person is being forced to learn things for myself. I wanted to become healthy and a better person, so I knew I would do whatever it took.

But I am hopeful that God will use me to help others to come to their senses and find the one who sets us free—Jesus Christ. In a later chapter I will tell you about my unusual encounter with God and how He changed my life. I will say that it's not a one-sided relationship. The relationship I have with God is mutual and that makes all the difference in the world.

Toxic Behaviors

While I was working at the safe house here in my local area, I would consistently take a lady to an AA meeting where I would sit in the audience and listen to the lead speaker. Every time I was there I would think to myself, if it weren't for the grace of God, I would be on stage talking to the crowd myself. I didn't see that much of a difference between my life's story and theirs. The main difference that I did see was that I escaped being addicted to alcohol or drugs. Fortunately, I was not caught in the throes of addiction.

At one point, however, alcohol did control my life. It served as the catalyst for a lot of the crazy things that I had done. My husband and I made a conscious choice that alcohol was not going to dominate our lives. This is the best decision that we made for our family. As a result, my husband and I do not really drink much alcohol. We might have a drink on a special occasion, like a holiday or a birthday, but we never even had alcohol in our home from the time our kids were five to eighteen. We didn't want them around it, especially in the home. I know that they were exposed to it from their friends, but we wanted them to make their own choices once they moved from our home. Most of the people at the AA meetings mentioned numerous times that alcohol was just what their family did and it was always around the house. Their parents always drank, and it just became a sociable thing that seemed normal to them.

Becoming a Good Wife

This section is hard for me to write since I never felt like I was a good wife because of the things that I had done. Once I learned how to forgive myself, I was able to change the way I looked at myself and the way my husband looks at me. I no longer have to manipulate to get my way.

Once I learned how to eradicate my wrongful thinking, I recognized that I am a devoted wife who cares deeply for her husband.

As a young Christian, I did not think that I could ever compete with the woman described in Proverbs 31:10-31. How can anyone even come close to her? There is no perfect wife or mother. We have all fallen short on this because we all are sinners and imperfect, but we need to learn from our parents' mistakes, and even from our own mistakes. Even though this scripture was written a long time ago in a different era, the concepts still provide valuable insights.

I took a really good look at this chapter in the Bible, and I have come to conclude that it was written for someone who was giving advice on what to look for in a good wife and mom. It would be as if you were talking to a young man to advise him on what to look for in a potential wife. It says, "A wife of noble character who can find? She is worth far more than rubies." Of course, today we would use different language. We don't talk about someone having noble character, but we can recognize that this is something of value.

Thank God that I do not have to check off all those lists in the scripture, but I have attained a lot of the characteristics of a good wife. I am a precious jewel in the eyes of my husband and children and grandchildren. I am my husband's biggest cheerleader. I always make sure that he is taken care of with food and clothes. I have listened to his advice all of these years, even when he didn't think I did. I am my husband's helper and try to make his life easier by taking care of the things that I am good at in our home. I use the resources that we have to buy the things we need. Keith has always provided well for me, our children, and our grandchildren. In addition, we have helped so many single ladies who didn't have anywhere else to go. I don't know if that alone makes me a good wife, but it is one of the characteristics of the Proverbs 31 woman.

We all need to have compassion for others in need and work hard for our families. Our children see what we do and are watching our every move. We have to be the best that we can for them. Praying for our children is important, too! Prayer has always been a spiritual staple in my life. I received that trait from my Grandma Garczewski and my mom. Does that make me a good wife? I believe that it does. I think the key word here is good, not perfect.

My husband and I continue to strive to love each other with openness, humility, and honesty—even if it hurts a little bit. We talk often. Sometimes we have heated arguments, but mostly we just talk. We both have prayed for each other many times and that will never stop. I have been there for him during the roughest times of his own life. That's all you can do—be there for someone. When you make a commitment to stay together, you have to have an open and honest discussion about how you feel. A marriage should never be one sided. Keith and I have been married 40 years and, as I have stated earlier, the first ten years were rough. I am thankful that we got through them so that we can help those who are struggling now.

Do you struggle with doubts of being a Proverbs 31 woman? Do you think you will never measure up to this kind of woman? I didn't either. But as I write this, I know all of my imperfections do not matter to God. What matters is His love for me! He loves you no matter where you are in your life. Whether you are a new wife or a seasoned wife. His love for you surpasses anything you lack. Don't be so hard on yourself. Give yourself a pat on the back because you are you and you are doing the best you can. Mercy and grace can carry you a long way.

6

Overcoming the Victim Mentality

I realize in retrospect that while I was growing up I did not consider myself a victim. I believe this is common for anyone experiencing trauma, particularly as a child. As time went by and I started to realize how the bad experiences affected me, I recognized that I had a choice—I could continue to be a victim, or I could overcome the victim mentality. It took me many years to make the choice to move forward and not dwell on what happened to me.

The term "victim mentality" carries the idea that one is always a victim. This individual believes that bad things will always happen to them. Sometimes people use the victim mentality as a crutch so that they do not have to own up to the things that they possibly have done themselves. Some people just use it as an excuse to get attention. I know people who continue to rehash specific things that have happened to them, over and over again. They just cannot get past the pain. I have been guilty of all this at times.

I remember a situation when I was fifty years old that showed me how I continued to view myself as a victim, even though I was an adult. My sister Louise and I went to visit our stepdad, Bud, at the hospital. Our mother was already there. As we were walking down the hallway to go to the cafeteria for a milkshake (they had the best milkshakes!), something caught my attention. I was accustomed to being very aware of my surroundings because I always had to have an exit plan. To my surprise, I spotted our biological dad standing in one of the patient rooms! We didn't know it but our Grandma Schofield, his mom, was in the same hospital.

Seeing our real dad really startled both Louise and me. Since the time that he left our mom, the entire family—particularly both our dad and stepdad—had NEVER been together. The two men did not get along and we feared that a meeting of the two would become explosive. In fact, my mom had no contact, even for a minute, with her first husband since she had married Bud. Realizing that both our dads were in the same building caused extreme anxiety in both of us.

This was also the first time in a long time that my sister had seen his mom—our grandma. We walked into her room and gave Grandma a hug. We talked for a little bit and then prayed for her. By this time in my life, that's what I did—prayed for everyone. We knew we had to get back to Bud's room, so we said our goodbyes and started heading towards the elevator.

As I hit the button to go down to the café to get our milkshakes, I leaned against the wall and tried to catch my breath. Louise and I just could not believe this was happening. My stepdad and real dad were on the same floor and all I could think was just terrible thoughts of what could happen if my stepdad found out. My stomach was in knots, and I had this sinking feeling that I was going to get into trouble—even at fifty years old! As I sunk to the floor, I said out loud, "When is this going to be over?" I have said that statement a few times in my life.

Because I always look for humor—even in tense situations—I found something funny that happened that day, too. We returned from getting our milkshakes and entered our stepdad's room when Mom walked up to us. She pointed to the divider as we walked in and said, "You both know Bill and Nancy, right?" We both stopped in our tracks. We felt as if we were in a time warp of some sort because my dad, who we just saw, is named Bill and his significant other is named Nancy. As Mom pulled back the curtain, we were expecting my dad and his girlfriend, but there was a different Bill and Nancy standing there! A friend of my stepdad and his wife Nancy had come to visit. But seriously, what a coincidence.

This turn of events is amusing in retrospect, but it really wasn't funny at the time. I am pretty sure my face was as white as a ghost when Mom pulled back the curtain. I couldn't even talk coherently. I took Mom in the hallway to tell her what had just happened to Louise and me. She said that she could see that something was wrong but wasn't sure what had happened. We laugh about it now.

The events of that day when all my family were in the same building but still couldn't handle being in the same room, made me pray even harder that God would retore these relationships. I held onto hope that—one day—we could all be together in one place.

God would eventually answer my prayer, but that situation reminded me that I still had work to do on myself. When I look back at that emotion, it was just my way of trying to cope with the "what-ifs" that always crept into my mind. I did not know at that time, but I still held onto the victim mentality—the overwhelming sense that something else bad was going to happen to me.

The New Not-So-Normal

On March 22, 2014, our stepdad Bud passed away. This was a very sad day for all of us; however, there was also a sense of relief. At first, we all grieved and brought up some stories about him. But then we were able to start living our lives without the dysfunction we experienced for most of our lives.

We now had freedom to spend time with our mom. We had so much fun. My mom no longer had to worry about doing something with her daughters being upsetting to her husband. Bud was so insecure that every time my mom did anything without him, he was convinced she was cheating on him.

Believe it or not, it took some adjusting to learn how to live without him. My mom did not know how to socialize without him because he controlled everything she did. To be honest, none of us women knew what to do with our feelings. Because we had lived in fear for so long, my sisters, mom, and I developed an unhealthy co-dependency on each other. We were still very dependent on each other even though we each were married and had children and grandchildren. My good friend Judy once commented that she had never seen sisters who were so close. She came from a large family and her siblings loved each other very much, but they weren't involved in each other's lives to the degree that we were. Her observation stuck with me for a long time. (Many people have spoken into my life during different times, and I would just ponder their declarations in my heart until the right time would come for me to understand what they were saying. God always brought these things to mind at the perfect time.)

After Bud died, I remembered Judy's words. I began to recognize that individuals, even siblings, should not be this close. We knew too much about each other because we were always trying to protect each other. I had taken that role more seriously than anyone else. From a very young age I had become the mom. My sisters—and even my mother—always came to me for everything. At the time I didn't even see anything wrong with it, but I realized later that I never learned how to set boundaries when it came to my mom and sisters. In fact, an epiphany came to me that I never learned to set boundaries at all. For all of this time, I allowed everyone to walk all over me. Until last year, I had never said no to my mom—ever.

The more I tried to set boundaries, the more people resisted and said things to me that, in retrospect, were not true. I recognize now that some people learned how to manipulate me by telling me that I was being selfish, mean, or self-centered. As a result, I always said yes to everything I was asked to do. I recognized that saying yes all the time caused me to burn out. I identified the fact that I was unable to be good to anyone for anything. I allowed this cycle to happen in every relationship I had. I just did not know how to say "no," and it wasn't anyone's fault except my own. I held on to this pattern as a way to fight for control, but eventually I recognized that everyone controlled me. Sadly, even from the grave my stepdad kept a grip on us all.

As years have gone by, my sisters, Mom, and I have developed healthy boundaries with each other. We are more respectful of each other. We are still family and help each other but not to the degree of what we did before. I didn't even know it was unhealthy. I didn't recognize that we were all so dependent on each other that our thoughts and lives were completely intertwined.

I am very happy where we all are now in our relationships. We each own up to our part of the interaction without feelings of guilt that we "left a man behind," as they say in the military. We have become stronger and wiser. We can finally live our lives in freedom without the mentality that we are victims. We are free. As each day goes by, we are all learning to be somewhat normal for the first time in our lives, and it feels great. It's as if we are becoming reacquainted with each other. We each are on our own journey to being better people.

As we approach new situations and new circumstances, we leave room for our loved ones to make their own decisions and even make mistakes. Especially for me, I had to protect my family and I did it at all costs. But the new and improved "RoxAnn without an E" can now live without fear of abandonment, rejection, or offense.

I have finally won the war inside my head! I can say the word "no" lovingly and not feel guilty about it anymore. I love my mom and my sisters and—no matter what happens—I know that we can do all things through Christ who has given us all the strength. This has been our power to get us out of the victim mentality. This scripture has gotten me through so many things, and it is very powerful to me.

We can do nothing without Jesus. God has taken each of us and poured His love all over us and made something beautiful out of our lives!

My Hall of Fame

The ultimate test of my healing came years later. A miracle happened on May 7, 2017, in answer to a prayer I prayed as a 10-year-old girl. Forty-five years later, my entire family was together for the first time...ever.

Several months earlier, I received a letter in the mail that stated that I had been nominated into the Sports Hall of Fame for Lawrence County, PA. Mrs. Alberta Kelly nominated me—the same teacher who helped me to correct my name when I was sixteen. Mrs. Kelly would be used once more in my life to help and bring healing. The reason she nominated me was for all of my achievements in track and field, which she asserted was "35 years overdue." I was surprised to discover that my school district even had anything like this because I had never even heard of such an event.

When I told my husband Keith about the letter and the nomination, he said, "RoxAnn, this is really a big deal!" I was still processing this but was thrilled to be included. The only requirement to be inducted was to be present on the specified day. A big banquet was planned for May 7th of that year. Leading up to the event, a local newspaper reporter interviewed me. I pulled out all of my trophies, newspaper clippings, my State championship medal, and all of my other ribbons because it had been a long time since I had looked at them. They were up in the attic.

This brought back many memories, and some were not good. I remember every time my name would be in the newspaper—RoxAnn Schofield—my stepfather would actually flush the paper down the toilet! I think this made him upset that his name (Upperman) was not in the newspapers. It was, once again, another reminder of how much he disliked my dad. I later discovered that he was in fact proud of me, but his obsession with his insecurities gripped him so tightly and wouldn't let him let go. His display of anger every time I was recognized in the paper messed up my identity all over again because I just wanted to please him.

I found out that my dad Bill collected all of the newspaper clippings and he was very proud of me too, but I had no way of knowing it at the time.

I looked at all of the accomplishments as we pulled them out of the bins and gathered and dusted them all off. There were so many more trophies than I realized. We had them stored in the attic for lack of space in our house. Like opening an old time capsule, this was a part of me that seemed separate from my life now. It was crazy for me that I had accomplished so much. My name was in the newspapers once again but now it was RoxAnn (Schofield) Gallagher, and I was so proud of that name.

For the banquet, I had the opportunity to invite as many friends and family as I would like. As I was asking family to come to this event, I immediately invited my husband, my mom, my sisters, my children, and grandchildren, of course. My stepfather had died in 2014 so the door was open to invite my dad. What was about to happen would never have happened if my stepdad was alive because of the relationship my dad and he had.

I remember feeling so nervous because I had to talk in front of a large crowd. The emcee of the event was going to ask each candidate random questions. That alone gave me anxiety. I am the type of person that needs to have time before I am asked questions because I never know what's going to come out of my mouth. I admire those that can speak with ease. I think that the biggest excitement for me, however, was not the award that I was receiving but that there was going to be a chance for my parents to see each other again. That also gave me anxiety.

I didn't even know if my dad would come to the event. When I was younger and achieving all of these awards, my parents and stepdad never came to my track meets. I knew that they were proud of me at the time, but I didn't have the physical support.

Finally, after months of anticipation, the time arrived. Even though I was an emotional wreck that night, I just let things play out. I remember watching my family and all those I invited come into the auditorium and walk to their assigned seats. I was so nervous with excitement! It really was a special day. Then all of a sudden, my dad came in and took his seat. As I watched, my mom got up from her seat and headed towards my dad. They exchanged greetings and even though my mind should have been on what was happening on the stage, I couldn't keep my eyes off of what was happening down below.

I thought it would be easier for me to be there to break the ice between the two of them, but it couldn't have worked out any better than like you see at the end of a good movie. After we talked a little bit, my mom and dad hugged each other. I remember my dad saying, "Let bygones be bygones." At that moment it was a freeing time for him and for my mom. My mom's response indicated that she had forgiven my dad many years ago.

When the emcee kept asking questions about all that I had achieved, all I could do was to watch both of my parents. As my heart was racing a hundred miles an hour I kept thinking to myself, *Hey people, there is a bigger story here than anyone in this room would ever know!* My heart was full! I never thought that this day would ever come.

This get together was an answer to a little 10-year-old girl who had started to pray that God would bring us all back together. Even though this was not the fulfillment I expected, God knew and used this event forty-five years later to answer my prayer.

We took pictures to commemorate that day. There is one picture which stands out to me and is still on my refrigerator. It's one of my dad and mom with me in the middle. I always look at it with a big smile. It is a really good memory for me and a great day of healing for all of us. I am so grateful to Mrs. Kelly for nominating me, and I am honored to be nominated. That day filled a hole in my heart. I am grateful for people like her who have come into my life from the time I was a child.

Catching Up

Years ago, I did a devotional by Beth Moore called *Believing God*. As she went through each chapter, I had to answer questions. At the end of the devotional I had a timeline written down. I gasped as I looked at the paper and saw all the times that God was in my life when I didn't even know it.

One of the scriptures that has been close to my heart is when God says He will never leave you nor forsake you (Deut. 31:6). God says He will always be there for you, but sometimes it's we who are distant from him.

This verse helped me to heal in the areas of insecurity, not trusting people, doubt, unbelief, and abandonment, along with rejection issues. No matter what, I know that God is constant and consistent. He will never leave me.

I'm pleased to report that as I approach my sixtieth birthday, I am the healthiest I have ever been in my entire life. I am not sure why it took so long to catch up emotionally, and I certainly pray for those that are reading this book that they do not have to wait as long as I did.

7

Learning to Forgive

I remember the time in my life when I was at the breaking point. I was caught up in raising our children and doing all the things parents should do. I wanted so badly to put all of my past behind me so that I could give my children a better life than I had. I tried to go back to the origin of my religious upbringing, the Catholic Church, and take my children along with me because that's what my mom did. I went to confession and talked with the priest, but I never felt forgiven. Actually, I think that I felt worse. I had so much inside me that I had pushed way down deep. All of the pain, guilt, and shame began to resurface.

As I was standing in my living room one day, I cried out to God, "Please help me, I cannot live like this anymore." This was May of 1990. No one really knew the anguish that I was going through. Keith and I were trying to rebuild our relationship, but things were not looking good. I wanted things to work out but just didn't know what to do.

My neighbor across the street from me, Linda (who happens to be kind of related to us), was one of my best friends at the time. Her brother married my husband's sister, so all of our children had the same aunt and uncle. Even though the children were still in school, it was a really hot day. She asked if the children and I would want to go and get ice cream when they got home from school.

Of course, I said yes. I mean who doesn't say yes to ice cream, right? Who would have thought that an ice cream invitation would change the course of my life. After returning from the ice cream place, she invited me over to her house so that the kids could play. We had talked many times, but on this day she started to share with me something that I had never heard before. She said that Jesus could heal my brokenness. Those words resonated with me. She did not know much about me and definitely didn't know that I was crying out to God earlier that day! Now she had my attention. She mentioned that Jesus can forgive me of my sins and give me eternal life. She talked about how Jesus died on the cross for me and loved me no matter what my sin.

Linda asked me a very simple question, "Would you like to ask Jesus into your heart?" At this point in my life I felt as if I was out of options, so I said yes and agreed to let her pray with me. She prayed a little prayer and then asked me to repeat a prayer that she said that went something like this, "Jesus, thank you for dying on the cross for my sins. I know that I am a sinner and need your forgiveness. I want to turn from my sins. I now invite you to come into my heart and my life. I want to trust you as Lord and Savior. I know that you will never leave me nor forsake me. I want to live for you and with you eternally. In Jesus Name, Amen."

Wow! This prayer was so powerful to me. I know that she only said a few short sentences, but every word resonated in my broken heart. I sincerely meant every single word that I repeated after her. Even though these were words I had never heard before in this way, something in me started to change instantly. I felt a little lighter than I did before. A weight was lifted off of me just knowing that someone would not leave me no matter what I had done. The idea that Jesus would stay with me and never leave me was transformational.

I finally felt as if I had someone on my side. As the years went by, Jesus became my very best friend. He didn't immediately heal me of everything right away because, to be honest, I don't think I could have handled that kind of healing. But I now had an advocate that would help me in every step of my life.

I ended up staying at Linda's house a really long time. It was after 10:00 p.m. when we returned home. I just was so elated that JESUS FORGAVE ME OF MY SINS. For the first time in my life, I really felt that release. When I walked in the door I wanted to tell Keith about this because I was so happy. He was sleeping but woke up when I walked in. He asked if I had a nice time, and I started to tell him how Jesus forgave me of my sins. He was still half asleep but turned over and said, "That's nice honey." I laugh about this now because even though he was happy for me, he didn't really understand how our lives were about to change. I slept really well that night.

I started to go to church every Sunday. For three months I asked Keith to go with me, but he wasn't interested. He noticed a big difference in me, though, so now he was curious. Finally, in September of that year Keith came to church with the kids and me. The first time he attended he prayed the salvation prayer too! In retrospect, we find it a little ironic that May is his birthday month, and I said the prayer that month, and my birthday is in September—the same month he accepted his salvation.

Someone gave us Bibles, so we started to read scripture, go to church, and listen to countless messages. This was the first time I went to a different church than what I grew up in. I was so shocked to see how much the people there loved Jesus. They would sing and raise their hands. I was surprised that people like that existed! This began my journey of learning to love Jesus—and myself. I absolutely loved the music and the words of the songs. Because I love music and could relate to it, the words were healing to me.

I began to understand that God knew me so well that he would use ice cream, of all things, to bring me to him. Isn't that so cool? God knew me and He knew my name and He forgave me.

As I started to read scripture and learned how to pray, I became a sponge just soaking up as much as I could to know the Lord more. I could see a change in my thinking, and God was healing me from so many things. Many people do not come to God because they think they are unworthy due to their past, but all He really wants is a relationship. That was the difference for me.

I began using everything that I was learning to teach it to my family. I learned a lot of scriptures but three of them really stuck out to me. Of course, John 3:16 was a staple scripture about not perishing but having eternal life because of my decision to follow Christ. The second one was 1 John 4:19, "We love because he first loved us," and the third one was Ephesians 4:32, "Be kind to one another, tender-hearted, forgiving each other, just as God in Christ also has forgiven you."

As I started to grow and mature in the things of God, I began to learn about the last scripture. I knew this was something I needed to do because God calls us to forgive just as we have been forgiven. Eventually, this became easy for me to do. I am always forgiving those who offend me, even to this day.

The first thing I knew I needed to do was to forgive both my dads. I sent Dad Schofield a letter. I came to understand that unforgiveness kept me in chains, kept me from moving forward, and kept me from blessings. I have learned that just because someone offended me or hurt me, it doesn't diminish what they have done to me once I forgive them. We all have pains and hurts. It doesn't mean they got away with something. Forgiving someone sets you free and sometimes will set the offender free, so you both can heal. God is the judge not you. Believe me, I have had to ask for forgiveness for all the things I've mentioned in my book that I had done. I also had to forgive. We should always be doing both, constantly.

I also knew I needed to forgive Dad Upperman as well. As I did, my attitude toward him began to change. Even though it took some time, he recognized that something in me had changed. Mom told me that he said to her that he didn't know what to do with me because of this forgiveness. He said, "Well, I guess I will just have to love her back." This is why we forgive those who hurt us, it changes both individuals.

Through the course of my life people could not understand how I could love and forgive a man who terrorized me and my sisters. This is the exact reason—because Christ forgave me. That is the simplicity of this whole book. It's about forgiveness.

I will say, though, the biggest challenge was not forgiving all that had happened to me or forgiving others—my biggest challenge was forgiving myself. I didn't even know that was something I could do. The day that I forgave myself changed me too. Yes, God forgave me from all of my transgressions, but how do I forgive myself? I literally had to say the words out loud. It was probably the hardest prayer I had to pray. I listed all of my sins one by one and began to forgive myself for all of them.

The New and Improved Daddy Upperman

I would have to say that my stepdad Bud, even though he had all of those strongholds, was probably the toughest man that I know. But God used me to crack that shell. In 2009, Daddy Upperman also said the salvation prayer! I had prayed for this man so many times but still couldn't believe that God would use me to bring him to a saving knowledge of Jesus Christ. Knowing that Jesus loved him and forgave him for all of his sins changed him so much. He would call me and tell me that he was praying for me. He started to go to church with my mom, got baptized, and joined a church. God does work in mysterious ways. I am just so blessed to have witnessed that transformation in him as well.

After he died in May of 2014, I wrote a letter "to" him to express my feelings:

Letter to Dad Upperman (May 25, 2014)

Daddy Upperman,

I know that Friday when I came to your room by myself that it would be the last day I would ever see you here on earth. I am so glad that your last 24 hours you were not suffering or in pain, because that is all we wanted. You had been in the hospital so many times I guess that night when they called and said you had died, I knew it was true, but I was just in disbelief. I never got to go back one more time to say I love you. I know I was being selfish! Yes, you are in a better place now because you are with the Lord, and I am so glad to be a part of that!

Daddy, I saw you reaching for someone while you were dying and I just wish that you could have talked, to tell us who. Your death in the beginning was frightening. You were such a strong man and I know that you were fighting it. I will never forget the last hug we had and how you held me for what seemed like a very long time, but it was probably seconds. I thank God for that special time we had.

I hope you know that Mom never did any of those things you accused her of and that insecurity you had was just a lie from the enemy. I miss you so much and if you were here right now, you would make me laugh so hard. You are the strongest man I know. You gave life the biggest try every day. You always talked to me and the one time you said that you will pray for me was a reward I got to receive here on earth.

I have so many good memories of you that they outweigh the bad ones. You taught me how to farm, how to ride horses, a motorcycle, and a unicycle (that was the funniest day when you brought that home). You gave me a car, a snowmobile, minibikes; taught me how tend to horses and hatch chickens from eggs in an incubator, gather eggs, and to clean up horse manure and chicken poop. I learned about tools and shoveled out ditches so our sewage water would run properly. You taught me how to fix holes in cars and you rewarded me with one hundred dollars so I could buy stuff to go to college along with my stuffed Snoopy dog that you gave me. I learned to cut the grass. I worked hard and always have, but I also have your giving heart and would give the shirt off my back just like you would have. Yes, I learned to be strong and not let a man take advantage of me.

I also believe I taught you some things too. I taught you how to forgive, to trust in Jesus, to accept Him as your Savior. I miss you so much. I miss your craziness, but also the caring love you had for us three girls and our children and their children and your children from your first wife. I will miss you till I see you in heaven.

Thank you for loving me, taking me in, providing for me, and for making me your daughter. I remember you bringing me twinkies and pads when I started my period. I will never forget how you taught me how to camp, spot deer, and even hunt.

You are the reason I love ice cream so much. Thank you for teaching me how to water ski—it was so much fun! Thank you that you gave me the love for the outdoors and to look up at a starry night. Daddy, I will miss you always because a part of you is in me and it will never go away.

I am sorry that I cry myself to sleep sometimes and that I ache for your presence, just to say that Ellyana said this, or Emma did that, or to say Kevin and Kaleena are doing well.

When the bad things happen, what will I do now? I know you probably would tell me that it's beautiful in heaven and you are like that little boy on the red bike, or possibly you're meeting my children that I lost. Will you give my children I lost a hug and tell them I love them and will see them someday? I hope to make you proud. Dad, that's all I ever wanted to do. I love you Daddy and I miss you so incredibly much. I am sorry if I ever let you down and I promise that I will continue my faith and I will pick on someone else now so they can be saved, just like you.

I am going to Belgium, and I won't be afraid. You faced your fear head on, and I watched you die with courage and strength. I know you were scared but I also know, no matter what you did in your life, the moment you died Jesus was right there. I'm glad you're with your momma and grandmother and father and Aunt Dolly and Uncle Rudy and all those that have passed away. I'm glad I will see you again and we will rejoice together with our God. So, for now I will praise and seek God, while you bask in the glory of God forever and ever! You were the best Dad and showed me how to forgive and how to love and how to always take care of family.

Enjoy the ride, Daddy—you and Jesus forever and ever!! You were loved always—unconditionally without regret. See, that's why I told you about Jesus. Can't wait to talk to you again and see you again. I will always be thinking about that day when I meet Jesus and get to see you again. Thank you for being my Daddy Upperman. And God, thank you that you saved our little family from Bessemer.

A New Beginning in the End

I am not the same person of thirty years ago. I have changed. I have always cared for people, but now I am able to help those who are struggling. I have been serving the Lord in so many areas inside and outside the church. I have probably served in every ministry in the church. I was voted "most versatile" in high school and those words came to fruition. I have done children's ministry, nursing home ministry, drama, chorus, worked the food bank, volunteered to count the tithes. I have painted, cleaned, and served many local communities.

What interests me most at this point in my life is Women's Ministry. I have led many Bible studies. I am always looking for that one person who might need help to get through. I can do these things because I know without a doubt that prayer works and that God is real. He is able to do so much more than I could ever imagine. I am always looking to help people in any way that I can.

I went to ministry school for nine months to learn even more. I have been on the streets helping the homeless and helping those who are lost and just need to find Jesus. I don't say these things to boast about all that I have done. I say these things because I get to do these things for Jesus. God doesn't want our works and what we do for Him. He wants us—period.

I have been told that I am a good wife, mom, grandmother, and friend. I would like to give all the honor back to God for helping me to achieve all of these things. Apart from Christ I cannot do anything. Jesus permeates every part of my mind, soul, and heart.

I am grateful to have been able to write this book, and of course through writing it God outdid himself again. This book propelled my healing more than I could have imagined. I pray for those that have read to this point. May God bless you and keep you. May His face shine upon you and give you peace. With love from RoxAnn without an "e".

8

Final Thoughts

Are you currently in a situation where you feel trapped and cannot get out? Are you angry? Do you think that it is never going to end? Have you ever wondered where God is in all this? I have learned during the course of my life that the hand of God is always visible—even in these crazy circumstances—I just needed to look for Him.

Please understand that you are not alone. You have a chance to get the help now. I wish that I could go back in time and show my dad and mom a glimpse of what God could do in their lives. I wish that I could go back to when my stepdad was left at the juvenile detention center and his family abandoned him. I would have told them what I am telling you now—God loves you! It is plain and simple. He wants you to release all your hurt and pain to Him. He will carry your burdens and be the lifter of your head. God loves us beyond our wildest imaginations. We must trust that in our messy lives, He is in the process of showing us how to rely on Him for everything.

I no longer have to keep these "hidden secrets." I am no longer a victim to all that has happened to me and what I have done to myself. In the same way that my high school teacher Mrs. Kelly had a profound impact on my life, I want to help others, too. Even if I could help one other person, it would mean so much to me.

When my stepdad died, I was the last one to see him. He said, "I love you so much." I hugged him back and said, "I love you too." When he died in 2014, it left a hole in my heart. We had a great relationship when he died, but it wasn't always like that.

You can have a normal life but remember…it's your life and it's not going to look like anyone else's life. No one is exempt from pain, and no one is exempt from getting hurt. We all live in an imperfect world.

Today I thank God for all those that He has placed in my life and how He orchestrated everything…even the writing of this book.

About Fear

As situations come up in my life, I have to ask myself, is this rational thinking or am I being irrational? For example, when I walk into a restaurant or a store, I look at my surroundings, slip into a seat, and assess whether or not I am safe. To this day, I cannot go into a place without formulating an escape plan in my mind. If somebody were to come in with a gun or a crazy person start to act irrational, I would have a plan. I can never let my guard down. Of course, once I am settled in and feel comfortable and safe, I have a really good time.

My whole reasoning for this book is to tell my story and provide hope to others who face crazy situations like my family had to go through. I believe that all that I went through as a child has prepared me for this time to sit and write all of this down and to help someone to know that they are not alone. God does not waste anything. Also, it's my choice to help other women suffering from anxiety, depression, PTSD, abandonment issues, self-image, rejection, and strongholds that keep them from moving forward. I know what they are going through, and who better to help someone than one who has already gone through it. Unfortunately, in order to share the good things God has helped me through, I needed to walk you through the bad.

This crisis of fear that I had to overcome was not easy. Even now, a situation will trigger something from my past. I have learned to recognize strongholds as dysfunctional ways of thinking. The fear of death, abandonment, and being sexually abused caused my mind to be very twisted. I've had to learn new ways to think and process information.

Early in my marriage, my husband went to our room to get his shotgun out to clean it. I just ran out of the house! I didn't even know why. Later I came to understand that the sound of a gun being cocked is a trigger for me that sends me into flight. Now, when my husband pulls out any gun, he sweetly comes into the room and gives me a warning that he is taking out a gun to clean it or look at it. All of our guns are in a big safe, so I don't have to worry about them.

After my stepdad died in 2014, my sister Louise's husband Rick helped me to overcome my fear of guns. He taught me how to shoot one of my dad's guns, a 44-magnum pistol. Rick was a master sergeant and drill instructor in the military. Since he had taught others how to use them properly, he was able to show me how to hold the gun, aim the gun down range, click it into position, and shoot. I was so nervous; tears just ran down my face. After shooting the 44-magnum a few more times, I told Rick I was done. It was all I could handle at that point.

Even though my fear of guns isn't completely gone, I face my fear head on. My mom didn't even know that I had such a fear of guns. When I told her, she hugged me and said that she was so sorry. I am not completely healed of that fear, but each year I get better and better at it. My husband is great about taking me out to shoot and showing me how to use guns properly so I can get a better grip on that fear.

We all have rational fears—they are part of life. Some are afraid of flying in a plane, getting an illness, or being in a car accident. If you are a parent, I believe you are always worried about your children. I looked up the word fear and it states, according to Merriam-Webster, that it is an "unpleasant emotion caused by the belief that someone or something is dangerous, likely to cause pain, or a threat." Rational fears are healthy because they alert you to things which could be potentially dangerous or cause you pain.

Irrational fear, on the other hand, is like rational fears on steroids. My mom, sisters and I lived with a host of irrational fears for many years. It caused a lot of dysfunction in all of our lives. It has taken many years of counseling and prayer to help us overcome these fears.

About Sabotaging Myself

The chapter on self-sabotage is the hardest thing that I have ever had to write in my life. I do not think that I have ever seen the actual words on paper. I knew I had to tell my story because I do not want other women to go through the pain of having an abortion. Yes, it is a temporary solution, but you will be haunted by guilt and shame for a long time. I know now that it is very common for women to have abortions, but the cycle of destruction has become a pandemic itself. I don't think that the emotions women go through after the abortion are talked enough about. This happened to me forty years ago and I will never forget the guilt and shame I felt.

Even though these words are difficult to write—and I know some people will think poorly of me—someone else needs to hear these words. I am no longer a self-centered, angry little girl anymore. I got through this, and so can you. Healing has come in so many forms, but I never thought in a million years that this book would bring a deeper healing in my own life.

So, what can you learn from my mistakes? Have you had an abortion and thought that it was something you did, and now you just have to live with it for the rest of your life? Do you believe that you can live without being in denial of your little secret? It's a crazy secret that many women feel they need to keep to themselves. As I listen to the pro-choice arguments, I don't think people realize what they are doing when they kill an innocent life. If I could have had just one person tell me differently—or I would have had any support—I would have never gone through with the abortions.

Although these things are in the past and I can't change that, I know now that God had a different plan for the mess ups in my life. I can never look back to that old way of living and can't even fathom that possibility. Sometimes I can't even believe that was me. But please listen, because this is not the end of my story. This was actually the beginning of my story. This is where I had to make the decision to change because I could not do that on my own. I knew I needed someone who was way more powerful than my sins and would love me despite my sins.

When I accepted Jesus as the Lord and Savior of my life, I became a new person. I am not who I was. Today I am a better wife, mom, grandmother, sister, friend, and family member than I could possibly have ever been. I will tell you that it wasn't my doing—it was Jesus who changed my life forever.

Please know that you are not alone. I am aware that women who are being trafficked are often raped and end up having abortions. Some people might think nothing of what they did, but for those of you who feel the pain, there is hope. You can be rescued by a God who loves you very much.

Around this time, I wrote a song about the experiences of my sin, and the name of the song is "A Diamond." I wrote the words first on April 11, 1999, and on July 18, 2000, I wrote the melody. This song has been sung to a lot of women. I remember singing it with one of the pastors of our church while we were visiting nursing homes. He said the song reminded him of a little girl who received forgiveness. He had known nothing of my story.

A DIAMOND
written by RoxAnn Gallagher

Can I be beautiful again?
Will I have the freedom within?
When I look into the mirror, will I see . . .
A diamond cut so perfectly

This freedom comes by his stripes and his blood
The diamond is Jesus on the cross with his love
I've anguished and hurt and wondered why,
These feelings were inside of me
Jesus was there in the clouds of my despair
I looked and I looked but couldn't see him anywhere
It was dark, it was cloudy and the enemy you see
He was trying to take my joy from me.
(repeat chorus)
I looked into the mirror and reached out my arms
It was the face of God and I was unharmed
So the answer to the question that is written above,
He said "Yes, you are beautiful and Yes, you are loved."
The diamond that is cut so perfectly is Jesus Christ
    living within me,
it's Jesus Christ living within me.

I hope that you like the words and that they bring some hope to you. The words come from a place of forgiveness and healing and from the love of God. I didn't realize how this song would impact me and change how I looked at myself. My sister Morreen loves this song. I am hoping that the words will minister to you as well. I am grateful for people that have shown me unconditional love. I am especially grateful for my husband's unconditional love and for God's forgiveness and everlasting love towards me.

About Experiencing Trauma

Regardless of what trauma you have experienced. You can become healthy, too. But it takes hard work. The poem/song is about taking responsibility for your own actions.

It's human nature for us to want to blame everyone else and not accept our own faults that live deep within our hearts. How do you move forward? I am so grateful that I can share this with you, my dear reader, and I pray that you don't have to wait as long as I did to realize I was a victim and could get help. I pray that you will get the help sooner than later. I pray you will own up to your mistakes and move forward. This world would be a better place if we all just took responsibility for our actions.

BUT NEVER IT WAS I
written by RoxAnn Gallagher

Nobody takes responsibility for their actions anymore
They take the blame and aim it right out the door
This world would be better off if we could accept our
    faults.
Knowing they lie deep within our own hearts.
It's you, it's her, it's him, it's them…But never it was I
It's you, it's her, it's him, it's them…Those words could
    touch the sky
It's you, it's her, it's him, it's them…It's how we reason
    why?
It's you, it's her, it's him, it's them…But never it was I,
    Never it was I.
A child was beaten, A husband cheatin', we ask why oh
    why?
A man in prison sits and wonders why he shot that guy?
We blame our parents, teachers, family, and our friends.
Because we feel it's easiest in the end
Let's just confess and we'll be out of this mess
Let's just confess and He will give us rest.

About Toxic Relationships

Have you found yourself in a toxic relationship? Are you the person who is toxic and do not know how to get out of that cycle? Do everything possible to get rid of that toxic stuff in your life. Pray to God and ask Him to help you. Ask Him to help you to become healthy and to forgive those who have harmed you. Please remember that just because you forgive someone, that does not mean that person got away with everything that they have done to you. Even though you let them off your hook, it doesn't mean that God lets them off of His. You forgive them because it sets YOU free.

"Do not be deceived: Bad company corrupts good morals" (1 Cor. 15:33 ESV).

"He who walks with wise men will be wise, but the companion of fools will suffer harm" (Proverbs 13:20 NASB).

"There is one who speaks rashly like the thrusts of a sword, but the tongue of the wise brings healing" (Proverbs 12:18 NASB).

"Do not repay anyone evil for evil. Be careful to do what is right in the eyes of everyone" (Romans 12:17).

Dear God,

Please help me to overcome the toxic relationships in my life. Help me to be more like Jesus in this area. I pray that you would give me wisdom and the ability to wisely choose who my friends are and relationships that will build me up. If I am unable to build up people right now, please send others who can help me do that. I know that I cannot remove myself from my family and/or people I work with, but I know that you can show me how to love unconditionally, even those who are toxic.

Remove any toxic things in my own life so that "the peace of God which transcends all understanding will guard my heart and my mind in Christ Jesus. Finally, whatever is true, whatever is noble, whatever is right, whatever is pure, whatever is lovely, whatever is admirable, if anything is excellent or praiseworthy, help me to think about these such things (Philippians 4:7). Amen

About Commitment

I came to realize that, particularly during our early years of marriage, I didn't trust anyone. I really did not even know the true meaning of commitment. I always thought that my husband would leave me because it is what I feared most. It was all I knew. After all, my father abandoned us to be raised by a man who abandoned his own children to be raised by yet another man.

When I made the decision to commit myself to the Lord in 1990, my life started to change for the better. I now wanted to follow Jesus with everything that I had. I learned that God is a God of first, second, and endless chances. I understood that I could completely start over after messing up my own life because Jesus risked everything for me. I learned how to commit to God and when I did that my life started to change in every area. I became emotionally, mentally, physically, and spiritually changed. But as I changed, the people around me changed as well.

As both of us learned about what Jesus had done for us and how to commit to Christ, we made a new commitment to each other. We were growing in the Lord and learning new ways to live. We both agreed to commit to our marriage and tried to be a good example for our children and our grandchildren in order to leave a legacy of what love really is. When I saw so many Christian friends getting a divorce, I realized that it's not just committing to Christ. It's also committing and choosing to commit to each other. That is exactly what Keith and I decided to do.

I remember my husband and I attending a marriage conference at our church. There was going to be a dinner afterwards and our friends were going too, so we thought it would be fun. It wasn't like a marriage counseling session but just informational. The various speakers that came brought wisdom and insight.

When we got back home, I remember discussing something that came up during the conference. One of the speakers asked, "What is one thing about your spouse that you have learned from them during the time that you have been married?" I remember telling Keith that I was so thankful that he taught me the word "commitment." The first eight years were pretty tough, but he never wavered on his end when it came to our relationship. He has always been the most supportive husband and father that I know. I know that because of his commitment towards me, it has given me a stability that I never had in my life.

Keith was able to forgive me and just love me like Jesus loves. It just amazes me how blessed I am to have both God and this wonderful man in my life.

My commitment to be a better wife became so much easier as time went on. It took a ton of pressure off of me when I was no longer weighed down under the shame or guilt of my sins. We have both seen other family members struggling with different things, and we are positive and pray for them. We have seen what God has done for us. If He can do this for us, then of course we believe He can do it for others as well.

Commitment from God gives you a base. It says in the Bible that Jesus is the cornerstone. And so when I think of that, the church and everyone in it relies on that. Jesus did not have to do anything, but He chose to commit His life even unto death. Now that's a commitment that no one can deny is impossible to do. But yet, He did that for us.

I started writing this song back in 2014, not for any reason other than the fact that God's love and what He has done for two young people, has made something really beautiful out of their lives. I finished it on June 16, 2020.

HOW CAN I KNOW THIS LOVE?
written by RoxAnn Gallagher

How can I know this love?
This kind of love your word speaks of.
How can I know this love?
This kind of love your word speaks of.

Your love is free, a GIFT to me.
It's so wide, so high and deep.
It's so long, it knows NO wrongs
How can I know this love?

It frees my soul, makes me whole
It is worth more than gold.
If only I could understand
How can I know this love?

Lord help me see your plans for me
The puzzle that is in your hands
Just a glimpse of wisdom please
How can I know this love?

It was on the cross you died for me
So, I would live eternally
ALL my life now I see
This kind of love your words speaks of
This kind of love your words speaks of

About Emotional Healing

What I have learned through the experience of writing this book is that everyone goes through the healing process in all different ways at different times. It's a type of grieving process. I can officially say, "Goodbye and good riddance, victim mentality. You no longer have that grip on me." I choose to love, and I choose Christ. The first step is to recognize that you have been sucked in by the unhealthy pattern of thought. This is the key.

Setting boundaries is so critical to your personal freedom. Many will try to manipulate you because you can't say "no"—even those who love you the most. I would urge you to pray and declare God's word over your life.

Declare God's truths to protect yourself against the lies of the enemy. Also, do not be so hard on yourself. Just keep pressing onward. Keep moving forward to being a better you so that you can be helpful to others.

About Toxic People

If you are married, your spouse may be that toxic person. Please, get yourself some help. Find a good church which preaches the Bible. Find people who have good, godly wisdom that can help you. And for goodness sake, avoid the toxic behaviors. Don't go to the bar with your single friends. Find healing for your inner soul.

If alcohol is a problem for you, this would be a good place to start. Alcohol has been the downfall of a lot of relationships. I believe that alcohol and drugs can exasperate already toxic relationships. If you have trauma and pain in your life, you may possibly be using this to cover up your pain without fully realizing it. We all know that it is just a temporary fix which only lasts for that moment.

I have a good friend who was facing a really hard time with a sick husband. The medicine he took caused him to be violent. This was the love of her life, but now she had to deal with this. She was caught in the middle of an impossible situation. Eventually, she had to remove herself from the situation because it caused her to be mentally and emotionally unhealthy—not to mention that her life was in danger.

One day she was walking and talking to God. She was looking for answers to this difficult situation. She asked God for a sign that He was watching over her and listening. As she walked through the woods, she was talking so loudly—basically screaming and getting it all out—that a tree fell right in front of her, seemingly out of nowhere! It wasn't raining or windy. She realized that day that, even though this situation was very hard on her, everything would be okay.

We are responsible for our own actions. We have to come to an agreement that we cannot fix toxic people. The only one who can help them is God. We did not cause this toxicity in their lives, and we cannot cure them. Only Jesus can save. He has way more resources than we could ever imagine.

About Forgiveness

I know some people still have so much unforgiveness in their lives. I just want to plea with you that it just causes physical stress and it holds you down so that you can't move or live. Sometimes this unforgiveness is so deep down that you don't even realize you have it. If someone has offended you, say out loud that you forgive them, even if you're not able to say it to their face. Because sometimes situations are such that you are not able to see that person because of their wrongdoings. But if you mouth the words out loud, you begin to be set free.

Don't allow someone else to keep you from living. Yes, we will not always forget. But when you forgive, you are setting yourself free. Sometimes you even have to forgive yourself. As I stated before, we are all imperfect people living in an imperfect world. But Jesus came to give us life and to give us life to the fullest. That doesn't always mean material possessions. But it means living with joy—true joy, not just happiness—in all situations.

I would like to make an appeal to all women who have struggled with trauma, caused by someone else or that you caused yourself. Jesus is waiting for you with open arms. He is not the same as our father's here on earth. He is perfect! He is our God! He loves you so much that He put His own life up on the cross to deliver you from your past, present, and future sins. I just want you to know that you do not have to be alone.

I believe this is my first of many books that I am going to write—God willing! I hope that the words in this book resonated something in your heart to search for help. There are so many places that you can go now to get the help you need. Find a church that preaches the living word of God. But most of all find God! He is the reason that I can get through my day. He is loving, compassionate, and slow to anger. He is not the angry God in the Old Testament. He is Jesus Christ who loves us so much.

As a matter of fact, when Jesus was ascending to heaven, He said that He was going to send an advocate and that was the Holy Spirit. Just like the wind, we can't see Him, but He is there in every step we take. It's our choice to follow. I was talking to my friend about free will the other day. We came to the conclusion that we are thankful for free will because why would we want to be a puppet on a string. This is why everyone is unique and different. We all are striving to be the best person that we can be, but in all honesty, we are not perfect. But that day will come when we are face to face with Jesus.

9

Life Lessons from RoxAnn without an "E"

1. Always love with everything you have.
2. Find someone who has the same beliefs and values as you do.
3. Find friends that encourage you and lift you up and make you a better person.
4. Make sure you have a servant's heart, no matter your status in life.
5. Family will hurt you. Just forgive them because you will hurt them too. (We are not perfect people.)
6. Be adventurous! There is so much that you can do, so many cultures, so much history to learn. Don't stay in your own little world. When you do this, it's always great to come back home.
7. Always check your motives to see why you do what you do.
8. Pray every day without ceasing.
9. Take care of yourself, exercise, and eat healthier foods. But don't starve yourself.
10. Please, on occasion, eat some chocolate or ice cream. It always makes you feel better, and you never know, it might change your life (wink wink).
11. Try to make good decisions because these types of choices will affect your whole life.

12. When you marry, make sure God is in the center of your relationship and always be committed to each other. It's a choice to stay with each other. Don't just throw in the towel so fast

13. Do not go to bed angry. You never know if it's your last day here on earth.

14. If you are a "flight person," go to a place that will be helpful to you so that you can stand your ground and work out the fear.

15. If you're a "freeze person," you are just one prayer away from moving forward.

16. If you're a "fight person," ask God to calm your heart and to soften it to be more like His.

17. Be teachable to grow in every area of your life.

18. Go on at least one international missions' trip! You are going to help others, but in reality, you are the one that begins life changes for the good! You will broaden your perspective and you are changed forever.

19. *Silence Treatment* are two very bad words and they hurt people deeply. Don't ever do that to them.

20. Be a leader, but also be humble to receive.

21. Always have mentors to help you and always let someone mentor you.

22. Laugh a lot, and I mean belly laughs! It's good medicine, probably the best medicine around.

23. Change your routine once in a while, surprise yourself.

24. Setting boundaries is good. It keeps you from being an enabler and keeps you from burnout.

25. Seek counsel without feeling shameful or guilty.

26. Forgive quickly and often.

27. Leave a legacy behind of love and life.

28. Ask God for wisdom and discernment in life's struggles and circumstances.
29. Always honor and respect your parents. (This will change your perspective on the word obey.)
30. Never settle. But when you know love, you will know that you know. Then give it everything that you can.
31. Commitment will go a long way in all areas of your life.
32. God first, spouse then family, and then others. (Keep this in order.) Believe me, this is so important.
33. Toxic relationships are heart wrenching. Be careful who you are hanging out with. You want to be in relationships that are positive and that speak life into you and make you a better person. Sometimes the truth may hurt!
34. God lives in you, NOT a building.
35. Trials will make you a stronger person. They will happen but how you handle them will make all the difference.
36. Yes, stop and smell the roses.
37. If you do not know "self-help," then learn about it and make a list to go to that place as much as you can to get rest.
38. Read your Bible. There is a lot of wisdom in it. It also keeps you on the right road, it challenges you, it shows you how much you are loved, and it shows you all the people from that book on what NOT to do. There are a lot of warnings in there.
39. Don't let FEAR keep you from doing what you love or that skill you are good at—because fear is a liar!!!

40. Showing signs of weakness doesn't mean you're weak; it shows how strong you really are.

41. Be genuine. People can see right through being fake. You will have a lot of friends if you are genuine because others can trust you.

42. You are responsible for your emotional, mental, physical, and spiritual aspects of your life, not anyone else.

43. Keep nuggets of truth in your life. For example, "God says 'I am God and you are NOT.'"

44. When you pray for someone, pray for them like they are your own family.

45. Parents make mistakes but so do you. Forgive often and don't give up.

46. As you awake every day, put one foot down and say "TRUST" and the other one down and say "OBEY." God, I will trust and obey.

47. Do not by any means ever eat yellow snow...haha!

48. Take every thought captive to Christ. Say to yourself, "Does this thought line up with the word of God?"

49. Be that person in a car, or anywhere, and sing as loud as you can. (Yep, that's me.)

50. If there is a person in your life that's always a thorn in your side, don't give up on them. Because that thorn will remind you how much you need Jesus, and it will teach you a whole new way of prayer. You will overcome by the blood of the Lamb and anything that is an obstacle you will learn to press through.

51. God is a miracle working God. His resources are unlimited.

52. Let go and let GOD.

53. Jehovah God has the final say.
54. A relationship with God is not one sided. You do your part and let God do His part. It makes that relationship work so much better.
55. Time does heal all wounds.
56. When raising your children, just do the best that you can because there is not a rule book on that.
57. If you are sitting beside someone in church, don't think that they know Jesus or have their life together. Strike up a conversation. You might find that they did not know Jesus and are a wreck (true story).
58. Women and men are different. (Don't try to change them.)
59. Seeing my grandchild being born was one of the best memories I could have had. (Thank you, Kaleena and Kevin, for that experience! It was healing for me.)
60. Age is just a number. You can do all things through Christ who gives you strength.

Above are just a few things that I have learned along the way and that I continue to learn. We will learn new things every day because every day comes and goes. Life goes on and we will have good days and bad days. Not everything that I wrote is written in stone and there can be some gray areas of course. But if this can help anyone, that is why I have written these life lessons. I pray that you will start your own list. I stopped at sixty only because that is how old I will be in September of 2021. The list could go on and on.

❦ Appendix ❦

Below are some resources for women who may find themselves in abusive situations. Please don't wait, reach out for help:

National Domestic Violence Hotline
(800) 799-7233

National Human Trafficking Hotline
1-888-373-7888

National Sexual Assault Hotline
(800) 656-4673

Substance Abuse and Mental Health Services Administration National Helpline
(800) 662-4357

Unplanned Pregnancy?

If you live in the Pittsburgh area and are struggling with an unplanned pregnancy, please contact:

East Liberty Women's Care Center
VISIT:114 N Highland Ave., Pittsburgh, PA 15206
CALL: (412) 956-5433
www.ELWCC.org

Contact the
🌿 Author 🌿

If this book impacted you, RoxAnn would love to hear from you! She can be reached at roxgallagher@gmail.com or follow her on Instagram @roxann_without_an_e.

Made in the USA
Middletown, DE
30 July 2023

35980705R00066